GOD'S IMAGE IN US

God's Image in Us

A MEDITATION ON CHRIST'S TEACHINGS

IN HIS SERMON ON THE MOUNT

by EDWARD N. WEST

Canon of the Cathedral Church of

St. John the Divine, New York

CLEVELAND AND NEW YORK

THE WORLD PUBLISHING COMPANY

Published by The World Publishing Company
2231 West 110th Street, Cleveland 2, Ohio

Published simultaneously in Canada by
Nelson, Foster & Scott Ltd.

Library of Congress Catalog Card Number: 60-5809

FIRST EDITION

Introduction

"When I read the New Testament," Kierkegaard wrote, "I get the impression that in God's opinion every man is a giant. . . . How ironical that every man is designed to be an Atlas, capable of bearing the weight of the world—and then to see what men we are; and alas, how sorry a thing it is that we ourselves are to blame for what we are!"

This is an honest appraisal of the Gospel by one who, though not inclined to overestimate the importance of free will, could always manage to recognize the necessity of man's response to God's promptings. This necessity must be kept in mind, or we are liable, in the interests of God's inevitably prior action, to ignore the reality of God's image in man. God, it should be noted, does not treat us as puppets; he treats us as persons. He even insists on treating us as being the kind of persons we ought to be instead of the kind we are.

Admittedly our freedom of will is not very great; but, feeble as it is, it is essential to our being persons. One

5

simple illustration may be helpful. The electric power which will light a room is brought there through cables from generators miles away. The room itself is wired, and there are bulbs in the sockets ready to light up when the power reaches them. Only one thing is necessary: somebody must flick the switch. When that is done all the pre-arranged parts of the system go into operation. It takes very little to set all of this in operation, but without that "little" the room is going to remain unlighted. It is the same with our free will and the power of the Spirit.

The Sermon on the Mount deals with every lamp and outlet, as it were, within the being it is ours to control, and it gives the directions for making "power" available. All we need to do is flick the switch—hear God and let the power of the Spirit work in us and through us. God insists, however, on lighting the whole house, even though there may be some areas where we don't want any light. The fuses, so to speak, won't stand for this division within us; every now and then we have to discipline our use of God's power to conform to his master plan. The power is constant and the directions completely adequate. All we have to do is let God's plan work. It doesn't take much strength; this, of course, is fortunate since we don't have much.

The Sermon on the Mount can make sense only to people who have already flicked this switch or are willing to risk doing so. In it Jesus presents to those who will listen the way of perfection. In doing so, his staggering knowledge of man makes itself felt. He knew what was left in man both of original sin and original righteousness; and even with this fullness of vision he was, as a good craftsman, content with the material with which he would have to work. This sermon is one of the clearest statements of Jesus' optimism about the possibilities of human nature.

In attempting to pursue some of the implications of the Sermon, I have taken the text exactly as it comes. I am not totally ignorant of some of the critical problems involved, but in view of the fact that most people read the Bible exactly as it is printed, it seemed to me wiser to ignore textual difficulties. In the first place, the very mention of them tends to confuse the layman; in the second place, the text, just as it stands, has stood the test of Christian living. It was this test which first entitled it to acceptance among the canonical books of the New Testament.

The Sermon still speaks. The words still have the ring of the voice of him who taught "as one having the right to."

ἐξεπλήσσοντο οἱ ὄχλοι ἐπὶ τῇ διδαχῇ αὐτοῦ·

ἦν γὰρ διδάσκων αὐτοὺς ὡς ἐξουσίαν ἔχων

The crowd were greatly struck by his teaching

For he taught them as one having the right to

The layman finds in the Sermon on the Mount a message which he believes to be particularly geared to his needs. Interestingly enough this is not only true of the layman who knows what the Sermon on the Mount really says. It applies equally to the layman who at best has only inherited conviction that the message is there, even though he does not know precisely what the message is. People can quote any number of versions of the Golden Rule, and sense that somehow this says something to them. And all of this in spite of the fact that the Golden Rule is not as simple a statement as, "Do unto others what you would have them do unto you."

The layman's instinct for straightforward language conveying relatively uncomplicated ideas has, through the centuries, made him distrust theologians who seemingly by-passed this straightforward statement of Christ. In fairness it should be said that most of the medieval "heresies" which originated with the laity derived basically from some earnest attempt to do exactly what the Lord told people to do, even as the "heresies" of theologians tended mostly to be drawn from the Revelation of St. John the Divine.

The layman, then, in reading the Sermon on the Mount, has had a suspicion that his Lord was somehow or other telling him to do something which, with Divine assistance, he might honestly expect to achieve. The late medieval arguments about faith and works tended to obscure this, and often gave the impression that Jesus issued nothing but counsels of perfection, which could not possibly be carried through anyway. The best one could do, according to such a theory, was to try hard and expect to get nowhere; or else not to try at all but to wait for God to provide such strength as was needed—even that strength by which God directly prompted the soul to take the first step toward him. Both of these latter views end up, I should like to insist, by making the precepts of Christ into mere pious observations on existence.

That this was not always the Church's theory is clear when we remember St. John Chrysostom's dictum: "No one should be depressed and give the false impression that the precepts of the Gospel are impossible or impracticable. God who has predestined the salvation of man has, of course, not laid commandments upon him with the intention of making him an offender because of their impracticability. No; but so that by their holiness and the necessity of them for a virtuous life they may be a blessing to us, as in this life so in eternity."

In practical terms the whole problem in understanding the Sermon on the Mount rests on what one takes the word "perfect" to mean. We are required to be perfect, the text tells us, because our Father in Heaven is perfect. Most of us have been brought up to think of the word "perfect" as describing a state of moral purity and spiritual sanctity identical with God's. If that, however, were what the word meant, then there would not be the slightest chance of anybody even approaching such perfection.

The word used in the Greek text means something quite different. It means "one who has reached the proper height of virtue and integrity." Its proper synonyms are "full-grown," "adult," "complete." If I, as an ordinary human being, am required, God helping me, to be my own most complete self because my Father in Heaven, whose image I bear, is his own complete self, then I am coping with an ideal that I can understand and which should control everything I do. In other words, if my problem is one of Godlike integrity rather than Godlike purity or rationality, then indeed I can be so thoroughly emboldened by the demands of Christ that I will have to do something about what he says. It is therefore worth my time to consider what man is as against what Christ says man can be. Christ's meeting with man in this way is always important. The "Good News," or Gospel, to cite only one example, tells what happened to ordinary men and women as the result of such an encounter.

Men walked with him and talked with him. Women ministered to his needs. Children flocked around him, and common people heard him gladly. The four Gospels, with varying details and from different points of view, describe this constant association. Indeed, the Early Church required of its Apostles that they should have witnessed this whole ministry of the Lord Jesus from the very day of his baptism until the day that he was taken up from them. This requirement is certainly still binding, but our encounter with Christ takes place in a different way.

It is no great matter to recognize Christ as the Eternal Word or the Wisdom of God. One can do this without any practical commitment whatever. The real problem lies in seeing in Jesus the brightness of the Almighty Father's face shining out on a lot of people just such as we.

Meditation on the Sermon on the Mount helps us to do this; it hits most of us right where we live. Collectively we can be a very unattractive lot. Often, when exposed to the insight of Jesus, we find ourselves to be even more unattractive than we thought we were; but also it must be remembered that, poor stuff though we may be, we are the stuff out of which the Kingdom is built, the basic material through which God has revealed himself.

Two

One cannot understand what Jesus is talking about unless one remembers that he was a Jew talking to Jews, and that he did so in a completely Jewish setting. The Jews had inherited the greatest religious tradition the world had ever known. There was a great ethical tradition and a great prophetic tradition, both of which were accepted by everybody. Jesus never had to take time out to explain that there was a God. Everybody agreed on that. The problem was: What was God like? He did not have to justify the Commandments of God given through Moses and the Prophets. Everybody accepted them as both true and given. The problem was: What did they mean? We can hear him truly only when we remember that the Jews of the first century were astonishingly like the Christians of the twentieth.

A few people had religion—John the Baptist was one. A large number of people knew a lot *about* religion—the Scribes and Pharisees, for example, did. But the overwhelming majority of the people, like us, had only an annoying bad conscience on the whole matter. They were repelled by the professionally religious—discouraged by the seeming irrelevance of religion to daily living, at least daily living for the likes of them.

It was all very well to take religion seriously if one could dress differently, and by general acceptance be expected to act differently, and thus be spared the temptations which beset ordinary men. But what of the people who had to earn their daily bread? People who had to pay taxes that were too high and live under the constant threat of war; people who had dull and unimportant jobs in life, who could not even earn their living if they bothered with the endless requirements of official religion. What had the Law and the Prophets to say to the great mass of unhappy and frustrated people of the day?

This certainly is not a problem exclusively of the first century. If anyone had to describe most of the people in our own day, one would have to admit that they, too, lead what Thoreau described as "lives of quiet desperation." How many really happy people do we know?—not only outside the Church, but even inside our churches? Is apostolic joy and enthusiasm the principal characteristic of even religious people?

It is trivial to condemn Christianity by the fatuous question: "If Christianity has been around for two thousand years, why do these problems still exist?" The problems still exist because man does not inherit his parents' ideas or beliefs. He is at very best only conditioned by them. God made me an individual in my own right, and my response to my God has got to be in my own right. Each generation has to be converted anew, and even if we could make the whole world Christian, this still would not insure the actions of the generation to follow.

It is not for nothing that the greatest religious thinkers of our age have insisted that an individual soul's relationship with its God is, like all love, a terribly intimate and private affair and in its own way unique. The crowd which hung on Jesus' words was made up of people who had not the slightest conviction that there was anything unique about themselves. Largely unloved by their fellow men and therefore equally unloving, they flocked around to see if this healer, whose reputation had rapidly spread throughout the cities and towns, had any words of healing to offer for the things which were bothering them. Hoping against hope, they followed him; and hope struck them where they lived.

And seeing the multitudes, he went up into a mountain: and when he was set, his disciples came unto him:

And he opened his mouth, and taught them, saying,

Blessed are the poor in spirit: for their's is the kingdom of heaven.

Blessed are they that mourn: for they shall be comforted.

Blessed are the meek: for they shall inherit the earth.

Blessed are they which do hunger and thirst after righteousness: for they shall be filled.

Blessed are the merciful: for they shall obtain mercy.

Blessed are the pure in heart: for they shall see God.

Blessed are the peacemakers: for they shall be called the children of God.

Blessed are they which are persecuted for righteousness'
sake: for their's is the kingdom of heaven.

We start to get the impact of these words if we remember that the word "blessed" to Jesus' listeners meant
"happy." It is easy enough for you and me to understand
that those who are persecuted for righteousness' sake
could be blessed, but are we really prepared to admit that
they could be described as happy because of it? Here are
all the poor, broken, gentle, tender things of the earth
exalted into the status of being the most important and
the most splendid. It does not really sound much like a
modern success story. Humility, concern, gentleness, passion for goodness, uncritical mercy, purity in heart, peacemaking—and even being persecuted for all of these things
—certainly do not constitute a very aggressive picture.
That they require a great deal of courage and a tremendous
amount of restraint anyone will admit; but do they fit into
our current conception of success?

Jesus, however, says that they constitute success and can
bring happiness; this is as alien to the Western way of life
as anything could be. It is, for instance, very difficult for
business people to see that there is a moral problem in
determining prices: whether to keep them down by good
management and methods or simply by mutual agreement.
Few of us have ever faced the simple fact that we may
possibly be paid quite as much as we are worth. Our
standards tend to get confused because we have defined
happiness in a different way.

And yet this is all the more astonishing when we remember that every worldly definition of happiness we

have known has turned to ashes in our mouths. We all know that in our day riches can guarantee nothing but taxes, that healthy competition can just as easily become unhealthy rivalry, and that frustration can produce ulcers equally well in palaces and prisons. Physical satisfaction has very largely produced nothing but physical dissatisfaction. Popularity makes for enemies and great position for outright hatred. Who, then, according to the world's standards is the happy man?

Nostalgically the world remembers the days of its innocence; it grants to the innocent inhabitants of an untroubled South Sea Island (if there is such a thing) the joy of living in an earthly Paradise. Such yearnings are quite nonsensical, because you and I are not innocent people; neither is anyone else. The simple fact is most men are unhappy men by their own standards. The crowd on the side of the Mount had good reason to be filled with amazement at Jesus' words: Happiness is to have love and be loved.

But any mature definition of love really cannot be arrived at without considering humility, concern, gentleness, passion for righteousness, uncritical mercy, purity of heart, peacemaking, and the willingness to suffer for them. The knowledge of being loved cannot be reached short of knowing a love which is personal, eternal, and, in the strict sense of the word, *real*. That, Jesus tells us, is what the *Kingdom* is all about.

Jesus, we notice, changes the ancient psalm phrase, "Blessed is the man" to "Blessed are they." The Kingdom had members; it began to count as part of itself even that crowd of strangers on the Mount, people who for the first time learned that their basic instinct and sense of values had some objective authority. They heard him, and as deep calls to deep, they knew he was right.

Three

Not only the multitudes were present on the Mount; the Disciples were also there. It is to his own Disciples that Jesus in a quiet voice gives yet another Beatitude:

Blessed are ye, when men shall revile you, and persecute you, and shall say all manner of evil against you falsely, for my sake.

Rejoice, and be exceeding glad: for great is your reward in heaven: for so persecuted they the prophets which were before you.

Most of the great prophets were, from the world's point of view, exceedingly unhappy men. They were hated by the great, distrusted by the mass of the people, and invariably persecuted and misinterpreted. With a few glowing exceptions, most of Israel's history had been an account of the endless war between the rulers of this world and the prophets of another.

Moses had been denied, betrayed, and even on occasion forgotten by the very people for whose liberty he had

sacrificed so much. Samuel's tremendous work had seemingly been worth nothing; at the end of his life there is
hardly any mention of him: this, it should be noted, was
the gratitude of a nation which God had fashioned
through him.

Elijah was hunted and pursued as though he were a
thief; and when the great Elisha died, it would seem that
few but the king gave him mention. It was the same with
almost all of them; they were great in their service to God,
but their very greatness invited enmity and persecution.

Even as Jesus' sermon was being preached, the great
John Baptist had succeeded in rousing the hatred of both
the secular and religious rulers of the nation. We can easily
understand how John managed to do this: his insistence on
baptism for everybody, as though all were coming from
paganism into true religion, did absolutely nothing to en-
dear him to those who thought that, being Jewish, they
already had all the religion anyone could have. John had
warned them that having Abraham for their father proved
exactly nothing, for God was able, out of the very stones,
to raise up children unto Abraham. At the same time John
publicly condemned the immorality of a civil ruler. Think
of the end of this great man—beheaded to pay off the
private social debt of a dissolute ruler.

A man once argued with Jesus over the persecution
which a prophet could face. The right argument would
have been over the possibility of being glad about it. For
the fundamental thing is not what the world does to us
but what we do to the world. It should be admitted however that gladness over persecution has caused the Church

considerable heart-searching for many centuries. There is certainly no doubt, for instance, that the early Christians so distrusted popularity that they often sought persecution for its own sake. If the world spoke well of them, they believed that this was due only to one of two things—either the world did not know them well enough to dislike them, or they had failed Christ and sold out to the world. Were they really and truly prophets, the world would simply not tolerate them. But there is this alternate point. Is there not something rather strange and possibly just a little diseased about the Early Church's craving for martyrdom? How, if at all, did these men and women differ from the masochists who we are taught to believe are neurotic? The answer, of course, lies in the fact that the persecution and martyrdom were borne for Jesus' sake, not for their own satisfaction or aggrandizement.

Tacitus, in his account of Nero's persecution, tells of some of the things the Christians faced: "Besides being put to death, they were made to serve as objects of amusement; they were clad in the hides of beasts and torn to death by dogs; others were crucified, others set on fire to serve to eliminate the darkness of the night." *The Martyrdom of Polycarp,* which even for that early age shows signs of the exaggeration that was later to discredit so many martyrs, still has an authentic picture of this aged saint. When Polycarp was brought to the stadium, a voice from heaven said to him: "Be strong, Polycarp, and play the man." (Words to be again made famous fourteen hundred years later in the case of Hugh Latimer and Nicholas Ridley.) The Proconsul urged the old man to curse Christ, and Polycarp answered: "Eighty and six years have I served him, and he hath done me no wrong; how then can I blaspheme my king, who saved me?" The Proconsul threatened him with wild beasts and then with fire. Polycarp answered: "Thou threatenest the fire that burns for an hour and in a little while is quenched; for thou knowest not of the fire of the judgment to come, the fire of the eternal punishment, reserved for the ungodly. But why delayest thou? Bring what thou wilt." When they were about to nail him to the stake, he said: "Let me be as I am. He that granted me to endure the fire will grant me also to remain at the pyre unmoved, without being secured with nails." The authenticity in this account comes through so thoroughly that the charge of masochism simply disappears. These men served their Lord with that mature calmness and solid conviction which is probably the authentic result of apostolic joy.

Just to suffer, we must notice, is not enough. Indeed, one can suffer and accomplish exactly nothing. The world is in fact full of such suffering, and it is part of the very tragedy of life. Pointless suffering may well move the hearts of others and thus save their souls, but surely there is a higher vocation for man than just that of being a pitiable object.

Suffering borne for Jesus' sake can still move us as nothing else will. Think of Kaj Munk daring to preach that series of sermons which so outraged the Nazis that he was eventually found in a gutter, full of lead. Or of Berggrav during the occupation of Norway, and Dibelius in East Berlin; of Patriarch Gavrilo and Bishop Nicholai, whose resistance to the Nazi thrust at Yugoslavia cost them thirteen months' solitary confinement, and Dachau for the duration of the war. Or of the numbers of French priests who disguised themselves as workmen so that they too could go with their people to the Nazi labor camps. Or of the natives of the South Seas who underwent torture and death because as Christians they would not betray the whereabouts of their white friends. This is the suffering that counts. It is facing death gladly at the right time for the right reason. No one can doubt the reward of such in the Kingdom of Heaven.

Four

Ye are the salt of the earth: but if the salt have lost his savour, wherewith shall it be salted? It is thenceforth good for nothing, but to be cast out, and to be trodden under foot of men.

Ye are the light of the world. A city that is set on an hill cannot be hid.

Neither do men light a candle, and put it under a bushel, but on a candlestick; and it giveth light unto all that are in the house.

Let your light so shine before men, that they may see your good works, and glorify your Father which is in heaven.

Too often we say of some man that he is the salt of the earth, meaning by it that he is rather crude, ill-mannered, and slightly stupid, but his heart is really in the right place. When Jesus called the people in front of him the salt of the earth he was using the phrase in a quite different sense. He was referring to the vocation of his people to preserve for all men the goodness of the world which God had made.

Nationally, vocations are very sensitive things, and most of us would recognize a number of great nations which, in the course of history, have been called on to do some important thing in the world. The terrifying common denominator, however, is that when each nation in turn effected what it was called to do and remembered only the pride and luxury which went with doing it, that nation either perished or ceased to matter. I say "terrifying" because we as a nation regard ourselves as a people with a vocation. We think of ourselves politically and economically as the salt of the earth; and with a not too thoughtful fusion of these two with religion, we often dare to think of ourselves as religiously the salt of the earth. All this is fine, and is probably very near being the exact fact. But Jesus' factual warning to his own people has certainly not lost its power. It is a fine thing to be the salt of the earth, but if salt loses its saltiness, what can make it salty again? If it has lost its saltiness, it is good for nothing after that but to be thrown out into the common highway, and *to be trodden under foot of men.*

His people were the light of the world, but to be the light of the world is to be awfully conspicuous. It is like building a city on top of a hill. It simply is not possible to hide it. You do not light a lamp in order to put it under a measuring bowl, but rather to give light to everybody in a room.

Jesus uses these pungent illustrations to lead up to his real point: if your vocation is to be the light of the world, then you ought to let your light so shine that the world will see what a good sort of people you are and glorify your Father in Heaven.

Most of us know the exact text of this passage in its full form. Yet how often we act as though the last phrase had not been added. One of my Quaker friends complains that his people are now famous for their secret deeds of kindness. The rest of us, were we equally honest, would have to admit that we time and again justify our religious and civil institutions because of their manifest good works. We give—we give generously—but we are naively hurt when others are not immediately grateful to us. If our good works are not done purely for the sake of showing people what our God is like, they cease to be good works.

Our most thoughtful leaders in both major political parties in this country are perturbed by the fact that we often manage to misinterpret ourselves abroad. In terms of economies we are ourselves a city, a city set on a hill. But we are actually something much more than that. We are a nation with a very generous heart. Yet we manage to do our charity very badly. We give where we ought to lend; we lend where we ought to give; we sometimes convey to people of less fortunate countries the idea that we are purchasing friendship, and at the same time we assure our own citizens that we are not really being generous at all, that this is just a way of keeping our own economy stable. Whatever one can say, it is manifestly clear that all of these different points of view cannot be true at one and the same time.

A city set on a hill is a standing invitation for stones to

be thrown at its windows. This is nothing new, and really should not amaze anyone. A rich person's generosity is often going to be misinterpreted. That, too, is nothing new. But somehow we seem to have failed in economic and political terms to convey to our far less powerful friends and neighbors the notion that as a people we believe genuinely in helping others to help themselves just for their own sake—because we as Americans place a high value on hard work, self-help, personal integrity. But if this be true of us as a nation, what will be the judgment of us as Christians? Our enemies say that we go into "pagan" lands for no purpose other than the ultimate exploitation of their peoples. Obviously we ourselves do not believe this, but from our thinking and our actions what else can others believe?

Africa is now involved in violent political growing pains, and neither the British nor we seem to have been able to convince the African that Western Christians went there for the sake of bringing men to glorify our Father in Heaven. What subtle snobbery has caused this? What unconscious condescension has conveyed to the African the notion that he was not only a "pagan" but also, God forgive us, inferior. I am not commenting on the situation in South Africa; we are not directly responsible for that. I refer to the areas where we have sent dedicated men and women to do missionary work for Christ. The tragedy of their situation starts to appear in its true light when these dedicated men and women come back from Africa and find it almost impossible to arouse the slightest interest of any American parish in individual Africans as human beings for whom Christ died: men and women capable, with God's help, of being *complete*.

Christian work in foreign missions has, then, little meaning for people; we should therefore look closer to home. What Gospel witness have we given for the Father's sake, say in the last six months, to set our light by our own good works on any of the following tragic concerns: juvenile delinquency, alcoholism, housing conditions, religious bigotry, anti-Semitism, race relations? The Christians of the fourth century held their processions out-of-doors marching through the midst of teeming, dirty cities. We hold most of ours nowadays indoors in immaculately kept church buildings.

Five

Think not that I am come to destroy the law, or the prophets: I am not come to destroy, but to fulfil.

For verily I say unto you, Till heaven and earth pass, one jot or one tittle shall in no wise pass from the law, till all be fulfilled.

Whosoever therefore shall break one of these least commandments, and shall teach men so, he shall be called the least in the kingdom of heaven: but whosoever shall do and teach them, the same shall be called great in the kingdom of heaven.

For I say unto you, That except your righteousness shall exceed the righteousness of the scribes and Pharisees, ye shall in no case enter into the kingdom of heaven.

Jesus makes clear he has not come to abolish the Law or the Prophets, but rather to bring out their full meaning. For him, as for everybody who preceded him, the Law and the Prophets had eternal validity. What he offered the people was his own principle for the proper observance

of the Law. It was, in strict Hebrew terms, his "way."
There were numbers of ways, but his particular way became known as the Way of the Nazarene.

His way was for him the right way to interpret the
Law and the Prophets; therefore, the right way to be a
genuinely religious person. Jesus differed not at all with
many of his contemporaries as to whether or not the Law
was binding. The question was, rather—How was the
Law to be observed? As long as there is a heaven and
earth, not the slightest thing shall be taken away from the
Law, not even of a letter or a bit of punctuation until
its whole purpose has come to completion.

There was to be no such thing as a satisfactory minimal
religion, a sort of partial version which would let you skin
by; the people who break the slightest rules and teach
other men to do so will be regarded as the most inferior
persons in the Kingdom of Heaven; but whoever both
teaches the full set of rules and follows them shall be
regarded as great in that Kingdom.

And now, for the first time, we observe the Lord's
irritation with the men who, from his point of view, made
a parody of religion. Most Christians have been raised with
a certain horror of the Pharisees. Because of Jesus' scathing
attack on their method of doing religion, it has become
easy to assume that all Judaism was Pharisaic, in the
modern sense of the word. The popular theory, held
until very recently, dismissed all Judaism since the first
century as a form of holy booklore, generally ethical and
often impressive, which however was in fact such hide-
bound legalism that there was not the slightest opportunity

for the Spirit of God to speak through a Jew in authentically religious terms.

In our own day, Martin Buber has managed to correct a large portion of this misunderstanding. Of course the charge leveled at Christians, as it has been for centuries, is that they too are hypocrites—exactly what Jesus called the Scribes and Pharisees. Christians do not like being called hypocrites; and often an extraordinarily sensitive person will avoid some perfectly genuine Christian commitment largely because he feels that since he is likely to bring some human weakness to it, it is probably better not to do it at all.

The word "hypocrite" is deserving of our attention, since Jesus uses it frequently. The word in classic Greek meant, "an interpreter, an actor, or a stage player." By the time the New Testament was written down it had come to have the additional connotation of "a dissembler." The notion that one is acting a part to the world at large, which in reality dissembles his real self and what he is like in private, is certainly not an attractive one. This, nevertheless, is almost the inevitable result of living by external rule, no matter how good, as opposed to living by an internal principle or discipline.

Our educational system, from start to finish, frequently tends to condition children into just such reactions. It is one thing to behave well in order to avoid being punished. But it is a totally different thing to behave well because this behavior accords with the inner dictates of one's heart and mind. Civil law does not produce the handsomer aspects of civilization, and in probably no other thing are we as inconsistent as in the handling of the ordinary rules of civilization.

Take our traffic laws as an example. Over a long holiday weekend a staggering number of traffic accidents usually occur. The immediate and inevitable American reaction is "There ought to be a law to take care of this so that it won't happen." The difficulty is that there is a law to take care of it. It is, however, a law which each man assumes is basically intended for somebody else rather than for himself.

One of my colleagues insists that he can learn almost all there is to know about a man's soul if he can see him behind the wheel of a car. Men who would never think of being rude in private company will lose their tempers and behave inexcusably when driving a vehicle. People who seem to be quite successful and mentally secure are suddenly seized by a compulsion which makes it impossible for them to drive behind another car for any considerable distance. Some terrible urge to get ahead betrays their curious weakness. The law for such people is an external discipline artificially imposed—one which must be obeyed only if one cannot safely get away with disobeying it. Genuinely secure people have no compulsion to push ahead. They do not have to prove anything to themselves. Indeed, the external law has become for them nothing other than a convenient expression of a considered internal discipline.

It is easy for people to attack Christians by calling them hypocrites. But hypocrisy is not a disease confined exclusively to religious people. The man who stands up for

a law which he personally has not the slightest intention
of obeying, unless forced to do so, is also in this unlovely
company. The person who recognizes any kind of double
standard is a hypocrite. But the real bite of our Lord's
attack on the religious leaders of his day was for a far more
specific reason than any of these. It was because the group
he was opposing set themselves up as leaders and then misled the people who followed them! The men who, in the
interests of religion, made religion unlovely; the men who,
in the interests of purity, made the average man believe
himself so hopelessly impure that he could do nothing
about it; the men who confused the Sabbath made for man
with man himself and got the order wrong; the people who
reduced the dread Majesty of Sinai to the level of a local
timeserving lawyer were the people who were really God's
enemies, although they were quite convinced that the outward motions would cover any responsibility they might
have. They regarded themselves and their opinions as
being perfect.

They drove men away from the love of God. That this
same criticism can still be applied to Christians is a tragic
fact of life. It is however the inevitable result when otherwise decent human beings start dealing with the person
of God as though, instead of being a person, he were in
reality nothing other than the definitive compilation of all
canon law. Human associations must of course have rules,
but the danger lies in assuming that these rules are
the same thing as the Commandments of God. Relaxing
the rules may well result in making one the very least in the
Kingdom of Heaven. But rationalizing the rules so that

they say exactly the reverse of what they were originally intended to mean can only end up by excluding such rationalizers from any part of the Kingdom. These poor creatures have, by their own rules, ruled themselves out.

Six

Ye have heard that it was said by them of old time, Thou shalt not kill; and whosoever shall kill shall be in danger of the judgment:

But I say unto you, That whosoever is angry with his brother without a cause shall be in danger of the judgment: and whosoever shall say to his brother, Raca, shall be in danger of the council: but whosoever shall say, Thou fool, shall be in danger of hell fire.

Therefore, if thou bring thy gift to the altar, and there rememberest that thy brother hath ought against thee;

Leave there thy gift before the altar, and go thy way; first to be reconciled to thy brother, and then come and offer thy gift.

Agree with thine adversary quickly, whiles thou art in the way with him; lest at any time the adversary deliver thee to the judge, and the judge deliver thee to the officer, and thou be cast into prison.

Verily I say unto thee, Thou shalt by no means come out thence, till thou hast paid the uttermost farthing.

The careful balancing of a crime with an appropriate punishment, all in one sentence, was the normal method of teaching the ethical law of Israel. It generally meant two sentences from Scripture were woven together into one legal statute. This was a normal enough way of thinking, but it invariably produced a quantitative measure of sin; that is to say, the seriousness of the punishment came to be regarded as the criterion of the heinousness of the crime.

Jesus would have no part of this. The underlying discipline which stops such killing is the complete avoidance of anger. Anger in the soul is the seed of murder. In God's eyes anger is as evil as murder is in men's eyes. The phrase "without a cause," absent from most manuscripts, seems to imply that there is occasionally an excuse for being angry. St. John Chrysostom points out that there is—when the matter does not concern our personal advantage.

The man who abuses his brother by saying "Raca" has, in God's eyes, committed a crime as wicked as the one for which men would give sentence of death. Whoever uses the violently abusive "Moreh" has, in God's eyes, done something as terrible as that ultimate blasphemy which in men's eyes could be punished adequately only by burning in the Valley of Hinnom.

Anger is so serious and so dangerous that we are not only responsible for our own but for our brother's as well. It is not as though we can go to the altar and offer our gift with the calm assurance that everything is all

right as long as we are in a happy frame of mind about
everybody else. Far from it. If we go to the altar and remember that our brother is angry with us, then our gift
is simply not offerable; we must first of all go and calm
him down. There is no such thing as a righteous grudge.

It is therefore of critical importance to us, as well as
to our brother, to recognize that peaceful, decent human
relations in all matters are far more important than the
question of either being right or seeming to be right. And
this carries through in all ordinary human relations. We
will row with a man over a small sum of money, and
instead of settling with him quietly out of court, we go
before some judge, lose the case, are sentenced, and not
only have to pay all the original sum, but the costs as
well. What sense is there in this? It isn't even practical,
quite apart from the fact that it is making a sum of money
more important than peace with our brother.

We have to remember the Beatitudes: it is the peacemakers who are happy.

Jesus, we can see from the text, is now gradually changing the basic application of his ethic. Instead of remain-
ing general, his teaching becomes more particular and
profoundly personal. He begins to speak of our own personal reaction to the things which irritate us. And what
is it that irritates an ordinary, fairly decent human being?
Our frank answer should be, Just about everything. It
includes being slighted or overlooked, being shoved aside,
being jealous or resentful of another's attainments, or
abilities, or recognition.

A person is certainly entitled to righteous indignation;

but the terrible problem I have to face is how much of my indignation is really righteous? Am I angry because a man struck a child, or because the man struck *my* child? Am I angry because a quite indifferent person was praised unduly, and was therefore praised dishonestly; or am I angry because the praise did not make it clear that I personally am very much smarter than the man who was praised? Am I angry when an animal is hurt, or am I angry when *my* dog is scratched by a cat which perhaps the dog has already frightened almost out of existence? Am I angry when another religious body pursues some line I do not happen to agree with, or am I angry because that religious body did not take my line, which I believe is manifestly superior? Am I angry because my country and all it stands for is unfairly attacked by another country, or am I angry because that country seems to be exerting more influence than mine in an area which does not belong to either one of us.

As I reflect on it, I have to admit that most of my righteous indignation is not righteous at all. It is just a way of combating evil with evil and feeling pious about it. The killing spirit is really a most unlovely one. It manifests itself in all sorts of disguises. Most men realize that they are not being angry enough to go out and kill somebody. But how often have most of us indulged the same basic feeling in other directions?

One of the most effective ways of killing ambition in youth is ridicule. One of the surest ways of destroying some potential rival's effectiveness is by calm and studied praise of the man—but always just short of being generous. We can with great ease twist circumstances and appearances so that they seem to imply a lack of morals or a lack of integrity in someone else. There is no more dangerous beginning to any conversation than, "He is one of my dearest friends, and I couldn't possibly like anybody in the world better than I like him, but . . ."

The killing spirit starts with anger—that jealous, personal hurt of the insecure, untrusting, unloving soul. If I am going to do anything about anger, I have to reflect on the Beatitudes, find out all over again what really matters, and reconsider what is worth getting angry about. I may be intelligent enough to realize that I cannot supplant anger with love by my own efforts alone just because I happen to be convinced it is a good idea; I also have to be honest enough to face the fact that God is not going to help me to do this unless I arrive at a pretty accurate assessment of what really matters in the Kingdom dominated by love. The final answer is only too clear: I have a perfect right to entertain righteous indignation and a deep sustaining rage, provided I am willing to give my life for the person who has caused my anger. Love always makes things hurt, but only love can take the hurt away.

Ye have heard that it was said by them of old time, Thou shalt not commit adultery:

But I say unto you, That whosoever looketh on a woman to lust after her hath committed adultery with her already in his heart.

And if thy right eye offend thee, pluck it out, and cast it from thee: for it is profitable for thee that one of thy members should perish, and not that thy whole body should be cast into hell.

And if thy right hand offend thee, cut it off, and cast it from thee: for it is profitable for thee that one of thy members should perish, and not that thy whole body should be cast into hell.

It hath been said, Whosoever shall put away his wife, let him give her a writing of divorcement:

But I say unto you, That whosoever shall put away his wife, saving for the cause of fornication, causeth her to

42

commit adultery: and whosoever shall marry her that is divorced committeth adultery.

Our world is still said to be a man's world, although American men are starting to have a shrewd suspicion that this is nothing but highly deceptive propaganda. Whatever the situation may be now, it is certain that the first century was a period when men dominated everything. We have to remember this if we are going to understand the group whom Jesus was addressing.

Marriage was a private rather than a public matter. A man took a wife with his father-in-law's consent. The wife's consent, while admittedly desirable, was in point of fact quite irrelevant. A woman's real dignity lay only in being a good wife and mother. Apart from that, she really did not have legal dignity, however great her influence might be (and one has only to read the tender passages of the Old Testament to understand how very great this influence could be). Under the law a man took a wife; and a man could with almost as much ease get rid of a wife by giving her a bill of divorcement.

On this basis it must be remembered that adultery could affect only women. An unmarried woman might get involved in sin either public or private, but not too much would happen, because no particular man's property had been damaged. It should also be noted that a woman could not divorce a man, on the somewhat unfortunate theory that property could not divorce its owner.

Certain Jewish schools of thought permitted divorce only for adultery or licentious conduct, and at least one

other great school of thought permitted divorce for almost any reason. In these respects it should not be too
hard for many of us to understand the most popular
general view of Hebrew ethics relating to marriage: a
thing cannot be wrong, we still say, unless their is a law
against it. There were admittedly very serious objections to
the women of Israel being involved in whoredom, but
apart from the women of Ammon and Moab and a few
other places, there was no legal objection to a man's enter-
ing into an immoral arrangement with a foreign woman.
A problem would arise only if he wished to marry her.

Jesus comments on the most rigorous popular interpretation of the divorce law, and in his customary fashion
makes it even more rigorous by referring the whole matter back to what goes on in the human heart. Adultery in
his teaching is wrong; divorce, except for adultery, is also
wrong because it will result in treating a human soul as
a chattel and force a woman to treat as temporary an
alliance which should have been lifelong; if she is not an
adulteress in the strict Hebrew sense, then forcing her to
marry again is going to make her one. Adultery, Jesus
teaches, starts in the mind. Apart from lust, there would
not be any problem at all: no lust—no adultery; no
adultery—no divorce. The chief thing that bothers the
layman about this statement is that there really is no
argument against it. Exceptions and allowances for hard-
ship cases may well have to be made, but no serious-
minded man really believes that there can be any other
basic personal ethic in this matter.

At a later point in this same Gospel in an argument

against the "laxist" view, Jesus gives them further insight into his mind in the matter. The Pharisees came and asked him this test question: *Is it lawful for a man to put away his wife for every cause?*

And he answered and said unto them: Have ye not read, that he which made them at the beginning, made them male and female.

And said, for this cause shall a man leave father and mother, and shall cleave to his wife: and they twain shall be one flesh?

Wherefore they are no more twain, but one flesh. What therefore God hath joined together, let not man put asunder.

Marriage is not something convenient—something which has been thought up by mankind; marriage is an association created by God himself. A man and woman in marriage are so bound together that they even cease to be separate people. They become a new person—a new, complete entity. All people will admit the validity of this as an ideal, and will even admit that in millions of instances it has been an ideal achieved: something with God's help made complete. But what about the exceptions? As the Pharisees themselves asked, *Why did Moses then command to give a writing of divorcement and to put her away?*

He said unto them, Moses because of the hardness of your hearts suffered you to put away your wives: but from the beginning it was not so.

Most obviously, in the beginning it had not been so; it was only when something went wrong that men had to be given a chance for the legal acceptance of some lower standard. But let us not deceive ourselves—it is a lower standard.

A man and woman have been married for twenty-five years; they have three children, and have had up to the present time a most happy home. There was not the slightest problem of coercion in the agreement to marry. Neither was under age. They were not too closely related. There was no problem about mistaken identity. Neither had any mental deficiency. Neither was insane. Neither was impotent nor sexually perverted nor ridden with venereal disease. Neither one had been engaged to another person at the time of marriage, and neither had any particular difficulties of personality to the point of making free consent impossible.

I mention all these things because any one of them might well have been an impediment to any real marriage in a Christian sense, no matter how long they have lived together or how many children they have had. Nothing like that however applies in this case.

This fifty-year-old man is suddenly enamored of a much younger woman, and wants to throw over all of his responsibilities and his sacred vows in the interests of some temporary satisfaction. Is Jesus really too rigorous with such a one as this? He is not being too hard. But we have to be completely certain that we assess the situation accurately.

Men have long accustomed themselves to the notion that women have a middle period in their lives when they are going to be strange and erratic, and need a lot of patient care. The usual theory is if the man can stick it through to the end of this change, then somehow everything will be all right. Most people seem ignorant of the fact that men, by and large, go through a similar change, and consequently suffer from a woeful recurrence of adolescence at such a time.

The man given as an example here may well not be a bad man at all. He is just suffering from an aberration which, God willing, will be only temporary. Obviously the man needs to be told the facts of life, and he may well need a physician just as much as a parson to help him through the period. But the day has gone by when we think of marriages as one-sided affairs. This man is going to need much patience from his wife, and she may well have to overlook a number of major or minor sins in order to preserve the integrity of the marriage. But before coming to a final evaluation of the matter, we should face the fact that physical adultery is nowadays relatively rare. It is at least still rare enough to be treated as news.

There are other and far more subtle forms of adultery which can do just as much damage. Their subtlety lies in the fact that they can so often be disguised as forms of good and worthy works. Adultery is "the state of something adulterated." To adulterate something means "to make impure by admixture of other or baser ingredients; to corrupt; to render counterfeit."

We talk a lot about the Christian home as a haven of blessing and peace, and we speak easily of the family as the first unit of any society, whether it be the Church or the nation. If all this be true, the activity in the larger community should then originate in the home, moving out from it in the sense of a blessing affectionately shared with others.

If, on the other hand, the larger units move in on the home, then something is being adulterated; something is mixed in which simply does not belong there. Viewed this way, we have to admit that there is always a possibility that the woman married to the man we have been talking about, having brought up the children and now having a large amount of freedom, may well have been neglecting her home, and her husband in particular, for a series of seemingly worth-while and useful causes. It is just as easy for a woman to let some worth-while volunteer work intrude as it is for a man to let his business worries intrude to the point of ruining the very home he is in business to maintain.

It is easy for a man, and particularly for a clergyman, to be critical of women's clubs, whether social or political, but church work itself can often break up a home as thoroughly and effectively as the most flagrant cases of physical adultery. What makes it all the more terrible is that there is a pious sanction given to this form of neglecting one's primary obligations. Bearing this in mind, we would have to know a lot more before we could be certain of just who is being condemned by our Lord's words.

We know very well what Jesus was like in handling individual sinners. The woman taken in adultery was more than just a test case to see if Jesus would agree with the Mosaic law—a law which required that she be stoned. No adulteress had been stoned for years. The important thing was that here was a woman who had been gotten at by lust. Some man's, yes, but her own as well. Now, to make clear to her accusers just how innocent they were in the matter of lust, he then let her go. He did not condemn her, but neither did he say that it was all right and did not matter, that she was just being human. He said: *Go and sin no more.* No tenderness for sinners must ever permit us to deny the horror of sin itself.

And I say unto you, Whosoever shall put away his wife, except it be for fornication, and marry another, committeth adultery: and whoso marrieth her which is put away doth commit adultery.

This is stern stuff, admittedly; yet no man, no matter how tragic his own life has been or how badly he may have messed it up, really would want anything else than Jesus' ideal for his son or his daughter. To interfere with God in his most complete image, the human family, is to indulge in the most terrible iconoclasm a human being can undertake. Decent people have always had a certain hesitancy about breaking up some object which others have venerated as a holy thing. Iconoclasm certainly has its proper place, and it may well be that some particular object has served only to get between God and man. Such an object may have to be broken, but the people who break it are taking upon themselves a most serious responsibility. In the course of its long history, Christianity itself has found it necessary to break up some objects or ideas. When the Canon of Holy Scripture was agreed on, for instance, a number of popular books had to be treated iconoclastically. These books were excluded from the category of sacred writing because they did not carry the authentic stamp of divine inspiration worked out in daily living.

Christianity's enemies have destroyed many things. The great library at Alexandria, which, were it still in existence, would double or triple our knowledge of the ancient world, was destroyed on the basis of the simple formula that if there were anything true in the books, that truth was already contained in the Koran, and if it was not in the Koran it was not true—so there was no point in saving any. Our churches have been desecrated and destroyed, and although the loss to the world of art may have been very great, the Church still manages to function without them. What has been built once can be built again.

The only icon which the Church must guard with passionate care is the human family. "Icon" is a Greek word for "image," but it means "image" in the sense that Jesus was the express image or icon of God. The human family is the living icon of the nature of God. It is one; it has one name; it has separate and distinct persons living in it. Yet each person partakes of that one name. There are different natures in it, but it is one entity.

The nature of God is love, and love must ever create by the very dictates of its own internal being. This is what the human family does. To attack the human family or to permit one's own family to be attacked, either by oneself or by another, is to be involved in the utter blasphemy.

In a strange reading of the text, but with a very sure insight, St. John Chrysostom, remarking on the plucking out of the eye and the cutting off of the right hand, says:

"Had he been speaking of members of the body, he would not have said it of one eye, nor of the right eye only, but of both. For he who is offended by his right eye, most evidently will incur the same evil by his left also. Why then did He mention the right eye, and add the hand? To show thee that not of limbs is he speaking, but of them who are near unto us. Thus, 'If,' saith he, 'thou so lovest any one, as though he were in stead of a right eye; if thou thinkest him so profitable to thee as to esteem him in the place of a hand, and he hurts thy soul; even these do thou cut off.' And see the emphasis; for he saith not, 'withdraw from him,' but to show the fullness of the separation, 'pluck it out,' saith he, 'and cast it from thee.' . . .

"But that thou mayest see yet more clearly the profit of this law; let us, if you please, try what hath been said, in the case of the body itself, by way of supposition. I mean, if choice were given, and thou must either, keeping thine eye, be cast into a pit and perish, or plucking it out, preserve the rest of thy body; wouldest thou not of course accept the latter? It is plain to everyone. For this were not to act as one hating the eye, but as one loving the rest of the body. This same reckoning do thou make with regard to men also and women: that if he who harms thee by his friendship should continue incurable, his being thus cut off will both free thee from all mischief, and he also will himself be delivered from the heavier charges, not having to answer for thy destruction along with his own evil deeds.

"Seest thou how full the law is of gentleness and tender

care, and that which seems to men in general to be sever-
ity, how much love towards man it discloses?"

It is important to remember that the Sermon on the
Mount was not a bit of gratuitous moralizing offered at a
Sunday School picnic. It was hard-hitting stuff for the
benefit of people right in front of Jesus, many of whom
had the very troubles he was talking about. That is why
people listened to the Sermon on the Mount. That is why
they still listen to it, centuries after it was delivered.

Eight

Again, ye have heard that it hath been said by them of old time, Thou shalt not forswear thyself, but shalt perform unto the Lord thine oaths:

But I say unto you, Swear not at all; neither by heaven; for it is God's throne:

Nor by the earth; for it is his footstool: neither by Jerusalem; for it is the city of the great King.

Neither shalt thou swear by thy head, because thou canst not make one hair white or black.

But let your communication be, Yea, yea; Nay, nay: for whatsoever is more than these cometh of evil.

The problem here is not one of profanity, but rather one of simple moral honesty. All truth is related to God, and as such does not have varying degrees. To consider one more binding than another is just to set up a series of internal qualifications as to the amount of security intended by one's promise. All oaths are binding and equally binding; but the question still is not that easy.

In our own day we solemnly hold people responsible for perjury if, after having sworn something to be so from personal knowledge, it turns out not to be so; there are serious penalties for people who perjure themselves. But even as a legal approach this seems a bit naive. If a man will take an oath and then lie, it is perfectly clear that the oath had no weight for the man at all. If an avowed atheist is required to take a legal oath, God helping him, what on earth does this mean? It may be an extraordinarily useful way for the law to catch up with people, but it certainly long ago ceased to have any meaning for people who were consciously perjuring themselves at that very short minute. The crime becomes actual only when the person is found out.

This is a far cry from the simple moral honesty required in the Sermon on the Mount. Moral honesty in personal terms means that if I say yes, I am bound quite as thoroughly as though I had sworn to do something; and if I say no, I am as completely obligated as though I had sworn not to do it. There is simply no question that Jesus' personal standards require my personal ethics to be straightforward and uncomplicated.

I stress the word "personal" because public oaths have always been of a different nature, and we have constant reference to God swearing by himself or binding himself by a voluntary oath as, for example, *the oath which he sware to our forefather, Abraham.* A private oath, on the other hand, was always of necessity promising something to God. To imagine that there were gradations in truth was simply to miss the nature of God completely.

In his bitter attack on the Scribes and Pharisees, Jesus pursues this matter of oaths:

Woe unto you, ye blind guides, which say, Whosoever shall swear by the temple, it is nothing; but whosoever shall swear by the gold of the temple, he is a debtor!

Ye fools, and blind: for whether is greater, the gold, or the temple that sanctifieth the gold?

And, Whosoever shall swear by the altar, it is nothing; but whosoever sweareth by the gift that is upon it, he is guilty.

Ye fools, and blind: for whether is greater, the gift, or the altar that sanctifieth the gift?

Whoso therefore shall swear by the altar, sweareth by it, and by all things thereon.

And whoso shall swear by the temple, sweareth by it, and by him that dwelleth therein.

And he that shall swear by heaven, sweareth by the throne of God, and by him that sitteth thereon.

Truth is truth: there is not the slightest difference between the temple and its gold or the altar and the offering made on it, the throne of God and God himself. The Oriental idea of truth was considerably different from that which we officially accept. The Oriental felt, with some justice, that so-called facts often tended to conceal truth, and that truth was often more accurately conveyed in parables than in supposedly accurate history.

Hyperbole is common to prophecy, poetry, and art. This is why prosaic and factual people often have such difficulties with poetry. Hyperbole is not just some form of wild exaggeration. Rather, it is a way of stating a case so that the case itself will receive adequate attention. These hyperboles enter the ordinary speech of exciting or excited people. We, as well as the Oriental, are capable of overstressing a case in order to make it clear. "Raining cats and dogs" was never really intended to be taken literally. The man who is "ready to lick his weight in wildcats" probably isn't, although admittedly he does feel well. The last time I was "scared to death"—I wasn't.

The problem naturally does not lie with such picturesque phrases as these. The problem lies, rather, in trying to attest to truth itself. One who tries to convince someone of something by saying, "I swear to you by everything I hold holy," has by that statement produced one or possibly two unfortunate pictures of human personality. His own character is sufficiently well known so that his ordinary "yes" would carry no conviction whatever, and perhaps the other person may be so like-minded that his ordinary "yes" would not be at all assuring.

Hyperbole in picturesque speech is one thing; but customary and habitual exaggeration is always self-defeating. The lurid jackets of popular editions of quite reputable authors are illustrations of this. Advertising, particularly of the dramatic arts, is notorious in this field. So many Class B pictures have been advertised as "colossal" and "epic-making" that one famous motion-picture producer is alleged to have said of a very bad picture, "It isn't even colossal." Insurance companies and most reputable businessmen nowadays are increasingly unhappy about any form of overselling. This is good.

It should be noted, however, that it is very easy to confuse frankness with truth. Frankness in far too many instances is nothing other than bad manners used with the conviction that they have divine sanction. Rudeness is always inexcusable. The old rules which forbade personal remarks and direct questions may have led to a considerable amount of circumambulatory rhetoric, but at least they kept numbers of sensitive people from being hurt. True frankness means an honest and straightforward answer done with affection and kindness to a question which was intended seriously. If a small boy approaches me, asking my opinion of a drawing which he assures me is a drawing of a cow, and if even with the utmost charity I cannot see in it anything other than something that looks like a celestial tea wagon, I am required to do some careful thinking before answering. In the first place, this is a small boy. This drawing represents the way he, as a small boy, sees things, and the only way he can, through his understandably limited talent, transfer this vision onto paper. With these two things in mind, I am required to give an answer which is encouraging, and if possible convey my real criticism by means of suggesting ways in which the drawing might be improved. To give the child any other kind of answer is to engage, even unconsciously, in the killing spirit. Ridicule does not help growth.

But the constant handling of truth as truth can impose an even more serious obligation on the person who is trying to take Jesus seriously. Some questions cannot be answered by a yes or no without causing grave damage to third persons. If I have just had a serious interview with some person, and another person asks me point-blank if the first one had come to see me about this particular serious problem, then I am forced to move into an area where I cannot say either yes or no.

Professional men are, of course, used to these questions, and most professionals and clergymen have developed various noncommittal forms for coping with them. My own standard response has come to be: "I spend a good portion of my life in private interviews involving professional communication. You don't really suppose that even if he had consulted me I would say yes." This answer is invariable, and would be given whether this person actually had come to see me or not. For obvious reasons, such an answer must be unvarying. The fact in the matter is that the second person had no right to ask the question.

The genuine obligation to truth is an obligation to a person—God—and not to a set of facts, even as I or someone else may happen to see them. No one is under obligation to answer a question from a person who has no right to ask it; but, on the other hand, we are all under obligation not to lie. It is essential to observe Jesus' own practice in this matter. Otherwise I might well be exposed to the charge of inventing a happy bit of casuistry to get me out of a tight place. When Jesus himself was approached by the Chief Priests and the Elders, they asked: By what authority he presumed to teach the people and who gave him this authority. Jesus answered: *I also will ask you one thing, which if ye tell me, I in like wise will tell you by what authority I do these things.*

The baptism of John, whence was it? from heaven, or of men?

This, of course, was an extraordinarily difficult question for them because if they said that John's baptism was from heaven, then Jesus would be in the happy position of saying, "Then why didn't you believe him?" If, on the other hand, they were to say that it was of men, then the people would be outraged, because the people all viewed John as a prophet. *And they answered Jesus, and said, We cannot tell. And he said unto them, Neither tell I you by what authority I do these things.*

Even in civil law the day has passed when any conscientious court will permit a witness to be bullied into a yes or no answer to a question which simply cannot be answered that way, if indeed it can be answered at all. The classic example, "Have you stopped beating your wife? Answer 'Yes' or 'No' " is now fortunately just a joke. But there was a day when this was not so. Even in traffic courts nowadays a person may plead guilty with explanation, and then the court is bound to hear the explanation.

This in turn, however, leads on to another very serious problem related to true or false witnesses. The Commandments absolutely forbade false witness against one's neighbor. As Jesus interprets the word "neighbor," this means false witness against anybody. But all human witness is partial at very best, and certainly in terms of personal ethics quite apart from any public ethics involved in a law court (even there, there may exist a very serious problem). All partial witness is basically false witness. I am fully aware of the fact that from a legal point of view circumstantial evidence is probably the nearest thing to accurate evidence there is, but most of the ablest district attorneys in this country and conscientious members of the various grand juries are aware of the fact that circumstantial evidence may prove exactly nothing. In personal terms, however, I can only take as a safeguard the simple fact that I do not know enough to assess the objective value of any circumstantial evidence. I do not see things the way God sees things. I do not know the actual facts God knows, and unless I can see and know this much, I am simply not able to judge anybody.

Therefore, truth, in terms of talking about other people, has to mean listing only those things which we know to be good, avoiding with the utmost care those things which on the surface seem to be bad. This is the only way that a Christian can avoid bearing false witness against his neighbor. It is worth mentioning that as a man gets older he discovers that the one phrase he uses the most, and which he finds to be the most honest, is "I simply don't know." The persistent habit of telling the truth is not going to make me into an objectively factual encyclopedia; rather, it is going to make me into a man deeply responsible to God for the honesty of my speech and my thinking.

Nine

Ye have heard that it hath been said, An eye for an eye, and a tooth for a tooth:

But I say unto you, That ye resist not evil: but whosoever shall smite thee on thy right cheek, turn to him the other also.

And if any man will sue thee at the law, and take away thy coat, let him have thy cloke also.

And whosoever shall compel thee to go a mile, go with him twain.

Give to him that asketh thee, and from him that would borrow of thee turn not thou away.

Ye have heard that it hath been said, Thou shalt love thy neighbour, and hate thine enemy.

But I say unto you, Love your enemies, bless them that curse you, do good to them that hate you, and pray for them which despitefully use you, and persecute you;

That ye may be the children of your Father which is in heaven: for he maketh his sun to rise on the evil and on *the good, and sendeth rain on the just and on the unjust.*

For if ye love them which love you, what reward have ye? do not even the publicans the same?

And if ye salute your brethren only, what do ye more than others? do not even the publicans so?

Be ye therefore perfect, even as your Father which is in heaven is perfect.

The two ancient rules governing relations with one's enemies would have made perfectly good sense to the aggregation of people whom Jesus was addressing. They all would have agreed that a man had a moral right to vengeance; and as for loving one's neighbor and hating one's enemy, this was just plain, good sense. One's neighbor was one's own countryman with one's own brand of religion; and one's enemy was a Gentile—a foreigner with a different brand of religion, if any.

Jesus takes these two standard and accepted statements and reinterprets them to describe the way an individual is supposed to behave. The whole problem of vengeance is a serious one. There are crimes which society simply cannot forgive—deeply personal crimes that hurt individuals. It is all very well to be critical of the Jews for believing that it was all right to drag some wicked man to law, and then to sit by and enjoy the sight of that man's being punished. But most of us are really not much different. I should like to be in the position of feeling superior to the rest of humanity on this matter, but unfortunately I find that almost the first thing that flicks through my mind when some hideous thing is reported is what would be the punishment appropriate for such a deed? Some wretched young man is reported to have kicked an old man to death. It is very hard to avoid the immediate reaction that probably the best possible thing would be to have the young man kicked to death, and in a way sufficiently public so that it would discourage other young men from attempting the same thing. That this wrong attitude on my part is not unique could be demonstrated over and over again in the course of Christian history. I forbear from criticizing the theologians of any other Communion, and only point out that as late as the seventeenth century first-class Anglican theologians were still suggesting that part of the joy of the blessed was watching the agony of the damned.

Obviously society has to take steps to protect itself, but it simply should not, in the course of protecting itself, commit the very crime for which an individual is being punished. Vengeance belongs to God. He can do all the repaying necessary. It is necessary that I make what I understand to be the point transparently clear, not for a moment implying that Jesus offered protection to people contemplating crime. The point, as I understand it, is that revenge on the part of an individual is in the long run suicidal for the human spirit. In terms of personal ethics —how we get along with other people—we should avoid petty rows. I remember years ago, as a young man, I became so angry in the course of an argument that I hit the young man with whom I was arguing. All he said was, "Apparently words fail you." The result was—and this might be expected—I did not hit him again. Indeed, I do not think ever in my life have I felt much more ashamed of myself than I did then.

The principle by which Jesus interprets the ordinary rules is a principle applicable to average people, and is not for a moment intended to cover absurd or even impossible cases. If an otherwise reasonable man sues you to recover a jacket to which he seems to think he has some legal claim, then if you give him your coat, to which he never thought he had the slightest claim, you will almost certainly have made a reasonable friend out of a reasonable enemy.

If someone bullies you into the equivalent of walking a mile with him, then on your own power do just as much all over again, and you will have destroyed a bully and found a friend. This is, of course, what St. Paul is talking about when he advises feeding a hungry enemy or giving drink to a thirsty enemy—*for in so doing thou shalt heap coals of fire on his head.* This is the way one overcomes evil with good.

Christian people are often very generous in giving others that ask, but most of us fall far short of generosity when it comes to our treatment of people who want to borrow. There are certainly some abiding rules for habitual borrowers also. Far too often they are just imposing on other people and avoiding the responsibility of preparing for things in advance. This all may be very tiresome and inexcusable in its own way. This, however, does not excuse us for our lack of generosity. Our standard of values is all wrong if any *thing* is to be regarded as more important

than human necessity. And human necessity can express itself in very strange ways. A young couple will be having
their very first dinner party in a new home. The bride is
most anxious to do well, and the groom is most anxious
that his friends should see the sort of thing he really likes.
They have no pictures. They have too much taste to put
up bad ones, and not enough money to own any good ones.
So, with the very best of intentions, the young husband
asks one of his friends if he may borrow one particular
painting.

The friend turns slightly pale at the thought. The painting is not only worth many thousands of dollars, but it is,
in the strict sense of the word, irreplaceable. Recognizing
fully all of the problems thus raised, if the friend refuses
to lend the picture, the one fact which stands out absolutely
clearly is this: however much he values his friend, the
young husband, it is less than that number of thousands
of dollars. The reader can object, and quite rightly, that
the young husband obviously has a slightly false sense of
values himself. He is making the false assumption that a
man's spiritual worth is expressed directly by the number
of fine things he owns or appears to own.

For numerous reasons, of course, the request should not
have been made in the first place; but Jesus is not at this
point talking about the rightness of the request. He is
talking about what we are supposed to do when the
request, however silly, is made. Possibly the right solution
would be to lend something quite fine with the specific
understanding that the young husband tell everybody that
this was a loan to warm up the house until such time as

they could replace it with something satisfactory. In this manner the man making the loan can both save his own soul, and also avoid damaging, even subconsciously, another man's integrity.

As for loving one's neighbor and hating one's enemy, the problem only becomes clear when the definition of "neighbor" comes into question. It is just as wrong to love Gentiles and hate Jews as it is to love Jews and hate Gentiles. And in personal terms, which is what this sermon is dealing with, it is morally suicidal to hate anybody.

One's immediate friends and relatives have always been entitled to special consideration. The resulting attitude, however, has more often than not been used to justify the worst aspects of nationalism as well as that utter concession to religious defeat known as bigotry. The ordinary rabbinic summary of Jesus' time stated that a man's obligation was to love God with all his heart, all his soul, all his strength, and all his mind, and to love his neighbor as himself. This was the summary which a young lawyer was forced to use as the reply to his own question: "Master, what shall I do to inherit eternal life?" Jesus agreed that this was correct, and told him to do it and he would live.

The lawyer, however, was not very happy about this solution. In the first place, it made him seem silly; and in the second place, it involved something which was an open question: just exactly who is one's neighbor?

Nowhere does Jesus' mastery of the parable show up more clearly than in the answer to this question. It is:

A certain man went down from Jerusalem to Jericho, and fell among thieves, which stripped him of his raiment, and wounded him, and departed, leaving him half dead.

And by chance there came down a certain priest that way: and when he saw him, he passed by on the other side.

And likewise a Levite, when he was at the place, came and looked on him, and passed by on the other side.

But a certain Samaritan, as he journeyed, came where he was: and when he saw him, he had compassion on him,

And went to him, and bound up his wounds, pouring in oil and wine, and set him on his own beast, and brought him to an inn, and took care of him.

And on the morrow when he departed, he took out two pence, and gave them to the host, and said unto him, Take care of him; and whatsoever thou spendest more, when I come again, I will repay thee.

Which now of these three, thinkest thou, was neighbour unto him that fell among the thieves?

And he said, He that shewed mercy on him. Then said Jesus unto him, Go, and do thou likewise.

It is not for nothing that Jesus chooses the examples he does. The laws in Leviticus specifically forbade a priest to have anything to do with a dead body, something understandable both religiously and psychologically as a requirement for a man whose first work in the world was to make offerings to God on behalf of people. Handling dead bodies and handling the sacred shewbread somehow did not seem to go together. The priest's fear of ceremonial defilement was so great that he could not risk the chance of the poor man's being dead. Thus service at the Mercy Seat prevents the man from showing mercy. This particular priest was not unique in this. A clergyman can very easily permit the rules to get between him and the very people the rules are supposed to help him serve.

The Levite was an even more tragic example. He was, in the strict sense of the word, religion's public servant. He was provided for by everyone else in order that he might do the work around the temple; but the Law itself regarded the Levite and the stranger equally entitled to the generosity of the people. The Levite, the stranger, the fatherless, and the widow were the first charges on the charity of God's people. Every rule of religion and every common loyalty should have served to arouse his interest in this tragic sight, but it did not.

One famous dean of a theological seminary used to say that the Levite came and looked on the man, and when he saw that he had *already* been robbed, he passed by on the other side. Christianity continues to have its own version of the Levite. Indeed, it could not accomplish its work in the world without him; but we would still have to admit that if an irreligious person makes his living from religion, the result is rarely going to prove helpful to afflicted people.

It was left for the despised stranger, the schismatic enemy, and doubly an enemy because remotely related, to show the compassion which should have been the very first works of the two champions of orthodox religion. The Samaritan had not the slightest reason to believe that the man he befriended would even have spoken to him civilly had there been no tragic happening. He knew nothing about the man, save that he was a Jew and therefore probably an enemy; he had not been asked to help; it was not his concern. Yet none of these factual reasons kept him from doing the work of God. He had compassion on him.

I have often envied Islam its constant use of the adjective "compassionate" in describing God. The word occurred frequently in the Old Testament, but rarely in the New, except when Jesus himself uses it. This word "compassion" is terribly important. It means "the ability to suffer along with another." It is the test, we ought to say, of all love.

If my neighbor, then, is anyone who responds when I need help, what about my enemy? The word "enemy" actually means, "one who is not a friend." On this basis we have to remember that all of us are bound to have enemies. I am sufficiently irritating to have a few who curse me, but I am not important enough to have many hate me; and I cannot honestly say that anybody treats me spitefully or persecutes me. But if this compassion of Christ really matters, then I am suddenly involved with some very real enemies. Some of my brethren are hated cordially, and some of my friends have suffered terrible persecution. I find it no problem to think well of people who do not happen to like me. We do not have to agree with those religious practitioners of our day who are always talking about the importance of being "accepted"; our problem isn't being *accepted*, it is *accepting*. And when it comes to this business of praying for those who have persecuted my friends, we come face to face with the splendidly outrageous demand of our Lord. When we remember that in another part of the world there exists a man just a few years younger than we, perhaps, but who is now completely broken in mind and body, a tragic wreck of a human being who was made this way for the joint crime of being violently Christian and basically pro-American, we find it very hard to come to terms with the demand that we pray for those who did this to him.

But Jesus is no sentimentalist. There is not a word which says that this sort of treatment is good, or that the wicked people who did this were really very nice if you got to know them. Indeed, we have every reason to believe that the better we get to know them, the more thoroughly would we disapprove of their every action.

The Early Church, too, had to face a similar problem. To bless Saul of Tarsus, to do good to him, and to pray for him certainly required a vast amount of realism both in obedience and in prayer. Saul persecuted the Church; he really persecuted it; he had men and women dragged off to prison because of their loyalty to Christ. He presided over the stoning of St. Stephen.

Here was an enemy in the fullest meaning of the word. To pray that the persecution would stop would not in honesty be praying for him; to say "For his own sake and for everybody else's I wish to God he'd drop dead" is not quite what Jesus means by praying for an enemy. Our Lord would have wanted us to pray with as much honesty as we could summon for the perfection of that man in God's way and in God's time. This haunting love of Christ, which Francis Thompson set forth so well in *The Hound of Heaven,* took Soul of Tarsus and dashed him down; but it also raised him up as the greatest of the Church's saints.

Two stanzas of John Ellerton's express this same theme:

O Wisdom ord'ring all things
    In order strong and sweet,
What nobler spoil was ever
    Cast at the Victor's feet?
What wiser master-builder
    E'er wrought at thine employ
Than he, till now so furious
    Thy building to destroy?

Lord, teach thy Church the lesson,
    Still in her darkest hour
Of weakness and of danger,
    To trust thy hidden power:
Thy grace by ways mysterious
    The wrath of man can bind,
And in thy boldest foeman
    Thy chosen saint can find.

Is this what I really want from my enemies? It is exactly what I must want if I am to realize my vocation of being completely myself: a recognizable child of the Father who is in Heaven. If I am going to be the child of such a Father, then I must, within my own limits, be like him. This is the only way I can be completely what I am supposed to be —perfect. Think of what God is like—the beauties of the earth and the sky are just as available to the bad as they are to the good; the gentle rain (the chief blessing in the Middle East) falls as much on the bad man's ground as on the good man's ground. God in effect loves all of his creation, and apparently judges it in terms of what it can be rather than what it is.

The best thing we ever manage to say about a son's resemblance is that "he is a chip off the old block." Possibly reverence will permit us to carry the analogy no further, but at least we must maintain strictly and honestly that there is no other definition of a godly man than that which means he is in his own humble, limited, human way like his God. For the perfection required of me means nothing less than that I shall, within my own infinitesimally petty sphere, be perfect: as broad in my compassion and tenderness in my whole being as God is broad in his compassion and tenderness in his entire existence. Anything short of this is toying with the Gospel.

Ten

Take heed that ye do not your alms before men, to be seen of them: otherwise ye have no reward of your Father which is in heaven.

Therefore when thou doest thine alms, do not sound a trumpet before thee, as the hypocrites do in the synagogues and in the streets, that they may have glory of men. Verily I say unto you, They have their reward.

But when thou doest alms, let not thy left hand know what thy right hand doeth:

That thine alms may be in secret: and thy Father which seeth in secret himself shall reward thee openly.

There is no religion in the world which does not extoll almsgiving in some form. That which modern man has come to call charity is, in its simplest form, the normal response of a generous heart. It is always rather touching to see some young father handing out cigars so that others may share in his happiness. The mere fact that neither he nor his friends even like cigars does not detract in the

73

slightest degree from everybody's pleasure—this is an accepted and agreed-upon form of expressing joy. Human joy goes much further than this, however; sudden good news, personal or national, will often be shared with total strangers.

In contrast, I must mention the situation in which many of my friends find themselves. Some of them are much smarter than I, yet they are forced to spend their lives at jobs which are not quite worthy of their talents. Some of them, through no fault of their own, are burdened with debts which will never give them a moment's ease. One man will be doing a superb job, yet no form of recognition is ever forthcoming. Another man, a gifted one, undergoes the daily torture of being responsible to a superior who certainly lacks good judgment, and, just possibly, integrity as well. Here is a young couple, just about to become financially comfortable, who suddenly are made responsible for a set of aged parents, one bedridden, the other senile. This means an end to camping trips with the children, to the possibility of buying a little house and pond in the country; it means the beginning of that tragic gnawing at the soul, that gnawing which hints over and over that nothing is going to be right until someone dies, and then it may be too late! Ministering charity to such as these is a fine art, if I am to help rather than to hurt.

Jesus was acutely conscious of the motives which prompt men to give. The obligation to give is not even debatable; the question is, rather, for whose benefit are we doing it? Just whom are we trying to impress? Our Lord's humorous illustration is so biting we tend to forget the humor. What a delicious thought!—having a trumpeter in attendance so that each time I give away a quarter, the general public's attention will be called to the action by an immediate rendition of Jeremiah Clark's Trumpet Tune, the organ accompaniment being provided by the crowd's deep-throated murmurs of admiration. The tragedy is that something much like this went on—and still does. Anonymous gifts are just as rare in the twentieth century as they were in the first. I wish I were in a position to be superior in this whole matter, but I am not. With shame I am forced to recall that my reaction to a recently published list of donations was one of annoyance—not Scriptural annoyance at alms disclosed, but, rather, the irritating suspicion that had I known the list was going to be printed, I might have given more!

But almsgiving to institutions, in our day of nationalized charity, is not as serious a problem as the personal giving we must do for our souls' sake. Consider the man who both deserves and needs recognition. I can of course start writing various colleges suggesting the bestowal of an honorary degree. I might even persuade my superior to take a hand in the matter. (I should point out that my superior really would not let himself be persuaded to do any such thing. He is far too wise!) Ultimately, because of my job, I might be in a position where a particular college was under some obligation to me: then I could really make a deal! All of this is fine; but how much of an honor is it? The man certainly deserves a degree, but not just any degree from just anywhere. The whole trouble is that I am trying to play God. An endless quiet speaking good of the man, an endless loving intercession for him, would permit the right thing to happen in the right way. Even with the best of intentions, one has to be careful not to confuse man's world with the Father's kingdom. The man I worry about is not himself worried at all; he knows perfectly well that his Father knows what he is doing. He has his reward.

The sharing of security is probably the heaviest call on our alms. My gifted friend who has a frustrating job needs the sense of being valued in spite of his job. At no point does Jesus speak with more careful warning than on the subject of doing good for men in such a way that the men themselves will not even suspect that they are being helped. It must be done with such quiet devotion and such utter lack of self-consciousness that even your left hand will not know what good thing your right hand is doing. The slightest whiff of condescension will ruin anything I might try to do for my friend. True, everybody will notice what a loyal friend I am, and my friend out of his loneliness will try to persuade himself that I really am such. I have had my reward. My friend is not helped; my God was never even involved in the enterprise.

But what of the young couple with the aged parents? I wish I knew. Certain things are, of course, clear. The couple has both integrity and pride. This rules out any such nonsense as a hidden Lady Bountiful approach. An unmarked envelope with ten dollars in it will upset both of them to the point of destroying any further contact with their community. They would wonder, and rightly, which of their friends regards them as paupers. Were they the only people in the country with such a problem, then there would be no difficulty whatever in coping with it. But the problem is so widespread that there simply is no easy solution. What then can we do? How can we help? Probably the best thing to do is (remembering Jesus' principles) the very hardest—casual visiting, asking them if they would be good enough to take your children out with theirs while you watch over the parents. Given space to maneuver, they will get by. They have a cross, and being decent people, they will carry it with distinction. The ministry of a loving heart is in such cases best done by a compassion which shares and cares, but never betrays itself. The only Person who ought to know, will. That is the only reward worth worrying about.

Eleven

And when thou prayest, thou shalt not be as the hypocrites are: for they love to pray standing in the synagogues and in the corners of the streets, that they may be seen of men. Verily I say unto you, They have their reward.

But thou, when thou prayest, enter into thy closet, and when thou hast shut thy door, pray to thy Father which is in secret; and thy Father which seeth in secret shall reward thee openly.

But when ye pray, use not vain repetitions, as the heathen do: for they think that they shall be heard for their much speaking.

Be not ye therefore like unto them: for your Father knoweth what things ye have need of, before ye ask him.

Piousness is a contagiously ugly sight. There is probably no other single thing which discourages the ordinary man's approach to religion so thoroughly as the thought that if he does anything about this religion business, he is bound to look sanctimonious. As one caustic wit has pointed out, it takes very little effort to be good among the really wicked, but it is almost impossible to avoid being bad in a company of people all of whom are bound for Abraham's bosom.

The impression of conscious goodness only inhibits other people. It certainly does nothing to commend goodness itself. There is, for example, no argument about a Christian's obligation to say grace before every meal; but it is quite possible to see people say grace in a public restaurant in so ostentatious a fashion as to make an Episcopalian wish he were a Quaker and a Quaker wish that he were not even there. The problem is never public religion in a public place, but rather private religion in a public place.

We always need to remind ourselves that Jesus conformed to all the basic public requirements laid upon Hebrew people. He wore, as did any other man of Israel, a phylactery. His only objection to the practice of wearing phylacteries was that some people wore very large ones for the sole purpose of conveying to others that their own personal holiness was proportionately greater.

Jesus wore the prescribed fringe on the bottom of his clothing. Indeed, this was the "hem of his garment" that the sick woman touched, believing that if she could but do this she would be healed; and it is a salutary thought that the fringes of religion—and let us be honest, they exist in all forms all the way from the vestments of highly ceremonial churches to the very austerities of Quaker benches—only serve their real purpose when they enable people to get near enough to Jesus to be healed. What

Jesus criticized was making the fringe deeper in order to make the wearer appear holier.

Jesus characteristically took the habits and customs of his people for granted, he accepted his people as they were; he was far too good a craftsman to complain either of his tools or his materials. It is ordinary people, just as they are, who are the stuff out of which God fashions the saints. Jesus took part in the synagogue services. He read lessons in them, preached, frequented the great Temple in Jerusalem, and faulted them only when they were less than what they should be.

It is important to remember that criticism of the public display of private religion is not an attack on public religion. If a man performs his private religion publicly, then he is probably doing it to be seen by the public. The public sees him, and he has his reward; he gets exactly what he wants. Private religion is something you do in your own private room when the door is shut and the Father alone sees you. The saints have invariably made it clear that the luxury of a private room is not always possible in this world, if by a room one means a separate area closed off by walls. They have, however, insisted that there is only one private room into which a man can always retreat: that room is the human heart.

The peace of God, which passeth all understanding, is more often than not something which a human being is going to know only in situations far removed from the popular definition of the word "peace." It has something to do with that inner serenity which comes from the conviction that no external thing can separate us from the love of God—*neither death, nor life, nor angels, nor principalities, nor powers, nor things present, nor things to come, nor height, nor depth, nor any other creature.* This is something which Christians have known on the battlefield and on the gallows. It is something supremely evident in the young man who was hanged on the center cross on the Friday before a Passover more than nineteen hundred years ago. Any meditation on that first Good Friday must ultimately conclude that the few words which were uttered from the Cross were glimpses into his private room at moments when the door was open.

Prayer, which is the chief occupation of private religion, is not just an endless asking of God for graces, virtues, and material things. It is, rather, the easy approach of a child to a loved and loving parent. Public prayer as it occurs in the liturgies of the churches is admittedly a very difficult matter. On the basis of Jesus' own words, liturgical prayer is not made to assume that God needs any information nor that he needs to be persuaded to do the kind or right thing by his people. Public prayer certainly assumes that it is public solely for the purpose of helping us as a group to understand what God has already purposed to do for us.

Liturgy in any real sense is the public work of responding corporately to the action of God. Private prayer is intimate talking with God, it is a conversation rather than a monologue; but it is a conversation made up of short, sharp, uninvolved petitions. The title "God" which Jesus uses is not the formal Hebrew word for "father," but rather the intimate Aramaic one which any child would use in ordinary, everyday language. The Aramaic word was *abba*.

It is not fair to imply that Israel was unaware of God as the divine Creator of the race. Nevertheless, even as strictly trained a Jew as St. Paul was surprised to discover that God had so put the spirit of his Son in his heart that he, too, could address God in this intimate and affectionate way. That it takes a certain boldness to address the power behind the Universe in this fashion should certainly be clear to anybody. We do it because Jesus taught us to do so, not because we thought it up all by ourselves.

After this manner therefore pray ye: Our Father which art in heaven, Hallowed by thy name.

Thy kingdom come. Thy will be done in earth, as it is in heaven.

Give us this day our daily bread.

And forgive us our debts, as we forgive our debtors.

And lead us not into temptation, but deliver us from evil: For thine is the kingdom, and the power, and the glory, for ever. Amen.

We are so accustomed to saying this prayer as a unit and to reading it or hearing it read as though it were a continuous composition that we tend to miss an important point. It would be impossible or certainly impracticable to hear this portion of Scripture read to us with long pauses in between the various petitions; but ideally considered, it might be done in that way.

Constant, adoring love of the Father, the endless speaking well of his name, is central to the requirements of Jesus. It is expressive of a son's love of his father rather than a subject's flattery of his king. Indeed, apart from using this customary Hebrew title for God when saying Israel's liturgic grace before meals, Jesus never addresses his Father by this title. But a good son to a good father is in the strict sense the imitation of God: this Jesus regards to be the true vocation of every human being. All of us are to some degree reflections of our own concepts of God. It is for this reason that Jesus uses analogy after analogy to make clear what the Father is really like.

The New Testament is notoriously unsentimental. One never encounters in it any such notion like the currently popular one that it really does not make any difference what kind of God a man believes in, just so long as he believes in some God. It is quite possible for a man to have so perverted his idea of God that in the name of his God he can quite conscientiously persecute other human beings. The least one can say is that such a God bears no possible resemblance to the Father of whom Jesus is speaking; and since action follows prayer just as surely as works follow faith, the true place of the Father shows forth in lives which do his progeny credit.

To pray for the extension of God's kingdom on earth only makes the full sense clear when we remember that the word "kingdom" means a sovereignty rather than a place. Too often we tend to assume that God is interested only in spiritual matters. With great ease we pray for wisdom or power, kindness or patience, but forget that salaries, schools, and jobs are of equal importance for the welfare of mankind. For me to pray for patience in my dealings with another human being who is impatient with me because I am making his job impossible is to miss the point of prayer and the point of God's sovereignty just about as thoroughly as one could.

To pray that the Father's will shall be done is to pray the prayer of utter, loving trust. It is not a stoic acceptance of the seemingly meaningless hardships of life; rather, it is an expression of confidence that the Father who wills good for all of his children can be trusted to see his will through. His will for Christians always includes a cross. But true Christians bear their crosses with such dash and splendor that we are convinced against every preconceived notion that these people really have joy. Indeed, Christianity has for centuries been so conscious of this requirement that it has absolutely refused to call any man a saint, no matter how much he suffered, unless he had a manifest joy. *Thy will be done* is not a concession of defeat. It is a voluntary alliance with a good thing for a good purpose.

To pray for our daily ration is, first, to admit that all we have comes from God. The religious realism of Israel took seriously the whole matter of feeding. Imagine a religion realistic enough to recognize that *The lions, roaring after their prey, do seek their meat from God.* Presumably human beings are expected to have a slightly greater sense of corporate responsibility than lions, so when we pray for our daily ration, the accent must fall very heavily on the word "our." It is obvious that if I eat well and my brother is starving, I have not prayed at all. It is equally obvious that the second helping of food which I do not need but which I eat anyway, is not going to arrive in India to aid some famine-stricken people.

I am part of a large company of people; I am a citizen of a great and rich nation. The government of my country is made up of public servants highly responsive to the will of the electorate. If the representatives from my part of the country, those who represent me and my immediate neighbors, are attempting to do something about a famine in India on the vast scale which only great nations can undertake, I owe them both private encouragement and public support. Far too often when they undertake some generous and statesmanlike action such as this, they are immediately attacked by people who say acidly, "Charity begins at home." To use Dorothy Sayers' phrase, "This shattering glimpse of the obvious really says nothing" —and almost less than nothing when one remembers that the other half of Sir Thomas Browne's original statement ("charity begins at home") was "is the voice of the world."

Obviously charity begins at home. Where else can it begin? The difficulty is it ceases to be charity if it ends there. To pray for daily bread means to take on conscious responsibility for daily bread—a most serious undertaking.

The rules about forgiveness are very simple. We have a right to ask the Father to forgive us our unmet obligations to him only when we have already forgiven others their unmet obligations to us.

For if ye forgive men their trespasses, your heavenly Father will also forgive you:

But if ye forgive not men their trespasses, neither will your Father forgive your trespasses.

The Psalmist accurately declared that God is to be feared *because* he is merciful. If God were to be so extreme as to mark what was done amiss, no one could abide it. But God is not. And if we are going to be like him to the extent of our poor, feeble abilities, then we too cannot be too fussy about ordinary human offenses. We should face the fact honestly that there are going to be offenses and that we are going to need forgiveness; but the sheer good news of this form of praying is that if we are honest and meet the requirement laid down, we can have some cause to hope for forgiveness.

For the modern man the problem is somehow a little more difficult. He finds it fairly easy to forgive others, chiefly because he values them so slightly that it does not make much difference what they do. They do not really get *near* him. His chief problem is to be able to accept forgiveness when every instinct of his sinful pride suggests that he was really too perfect to have committed the sin in the first place. The woeful discovery that he was not morally perfect comes to him as a staggering blow.

Of all the difficulties in the Lord's Prayer, there is nothing which confuses the layman as much as a prayer that the Father will not lead us into temptation. Because of our Western Christian attitudes, it is almost impossible for us to think in such strict Old Testament terms. For the Hebrew, God was the beginning and end of everything. God could send an evil spirit to trouble Saul. God could harden Pharaoh's heart. God could bring evil on his

people. God could specifically withhold Abimelech from
sin. Satan could come into the presence of God and even
argue with him. God could lead Jesus to the desert place
for the sole purpose of having him tested by the Devil. All
this is very strange to us, chiefly because we are not, as a
people, interested in the absolute primacy of God in everything. The Hebrew was a factual man, not in the slightest
degree interested in metaphysics. He couldn't care less
where evil came from. He had no doctrine of the Fall of
Man, and was not interested in the origin of the darkness
which always tried to swallow up light and extinguish it.
All these things were just facts of life, but they were facts
of life in a world which owed its origin to God. This may
be totally inadequate metaphysics, but it was very sound
religion. At least it resulted in a religion with one God
rather than the frequent Christian compromise which
results in two gods—one good one and one bad one.

Our naïveté in the matter becomes rather transparent
when we object loudly to God being even remotely responsible for the creation of any evil thing; and yet at the same
time have not the slighest question of his having created us.
For the Jew—and we must remember Jesus was a Jew
talking to Jews—it was perfectly appropriate to pray
God to lead us by a safer route than the one we would
be likely to choose for ourselves. This in fact is the Jewish
way of saying it—*Lead us not into temptation.*

This approach constitutes the prayerful avoidance of
taking on more than one can handle. Adolescents are
notorious for the ease with which they take on physical
and moral testing they are not up to, but even those of

us who are older are not always much smarter in the matter. A good teacher, a good psychiatrist, or a good physician may well have to explore some of the more tortuous paths of the human mind and absorb a large amount of quite horrifying information; but for others without their particular professional responsibilities to take on a good portion of this reading is just frankly to indulge in prurience, which the dictionary defines as "lascivious uneasiness or curiosity."

St. Paul is never more factual than when he says, *Be not deceived: evil communications corrupt good manners.* The Greek word for "manners" is *ethos,* the characteristic spirit, disposition, or tendency of a people. Bad language, bad habits, and bad morals are all contagious. Jesus could minister safely in a barroom; not all of his followers could be so successful. It is one thing to love a drunkard, but a totally different thing to get equally drunk just to prove to him that you love him. As practical people not primarily concerned with metaphysics we can well afford to pray the prayer just as it stands.

The Jews were equally factual on the subject of evil. There was for them no such thing as abstract evil any more than there was any such thing as abstract good. Good was God and evil was the Devil. In our own day when we know, or at least think we know, much more about personality, we can afford not to be shocked at the notion that evil is a self-propelled, self-determined intelligence, which is exactly what being a person means. Belief that there is a personal Devil is a perfectly reputable idea, provided one does not assume that in the word "person" there is an implication of horns, hoofs, and a tail. Indeed, the ancient enemy of our race is far more likely to attack us through second-class choices of good things. The young man and the young woman who want to live together before they are married are not acting on the basis of any desire for something basically wrong. Indeed, that which is implanted in them is an instinct given by God himself. The difficulty is that they will do the right thing the wrong way: therein lies the sin.

The man who desires to feed his children adequately certainly does not want a wrong thing. But a more serious problem arises if in the course of wanting this good thing, he finds that the easiest and most satisfactory way of acquiring the money for food is by stealing. As Shakespeare points out, "The devil can cite Scripture for his purpose. . . . O, what a goodly outside falsehood hath!"

The doxology with which St. Matthew's text concludes the Lord's Prayer is a beautiful one based on a popular Jewish model. It should be noted that there are many early copies of the Bible which do not include it, and also that no other Gospel includes it. The Vulgate Bible omits it, as does the Roman Catholic liturgy. St. John Chrysostom, writing in the latter part of the fourth century, accepts the doxology as a regular part of the text. Therefore, the liturgy of the Eastern Orthodox Church accepts it. The Anglican communion in general uses it at Holy Communion. The King James Version includes it, but the Revised Standard Version omits it with a note, "Other authorities, some ancient, add, in some form, *For thine is the kingdom* . . ." All this must be mentioned to be scrupulously fair to our religious friends and neighbors. That this doxology can be of profound religious significance is manifest from St. John Chrysostom's bold and deeply moving comment on it.

"Having then made us anxious as before conflict, by putting us in mind of the enemy, and having cut away from us all our remissness; He again encourages and raises our spirits, by bringing to our remembrance the King under whom we are arrayed, and signifying Him to be more powerful than all. 'For thine,' saith He, 'is the kingdom, and the power, and the glory.'

"Doth it not follow, that if His be the kingdom, we should fear no one, since there can be none to withstand, and divide the empire with him. For when He saith, 'Thine is the kingdom,' He sets before us even him, who is warring against us, brought into subjection, though he seem to oppose, God for a while permitting it. For in truth he too is among God's servants, though of the degraded class, and those guilty of offense; and he would not dare set upon any of his fellow servants, had he not first received license from above. And why say I, 'his fellow servants'? Not even against swine did he venture any outrage, until He Himself allowed him; nor against flocks, nor herds, until he had received permission from above.

" 'And the power,' saith he. Therefore, manifold as thy weakness may be, thou mayest of right be confident, having such a one to reign over thee, who is able fully to accomplish all, and that with ease, even by thee.

" 'And the glory, for ever. Amen.' Thus He not only frees thee from the dangers that are approaching thee, but can make thee also glorious and illustrious. For as His power is great, so also is His glory unspeakable, and they are all boundless, and no end of them. Seest thou how He hath by every means anointed His Champion, and hath framed Him to be full of confidence?"

Twelve

Lay not up for yourselves treasures upon earth, where moth and rust doth corrupt, and where thieves break through and steal:

But lay up for yourselves treasures in heaven, where neither moth nor rust doth corrupt, and where thieves do not break through nor steal:

For where your treasure is, there will your heart be also.

Oriental wealth consisted very largely of fine clothing, steel weapons, silver, gold, and gems. All of them were subject to certain possible fates in this world: moths could destroy the clothing; rust could ruin the steel; and thieves could carry off gold, silver, and gems.

Our riches are somewhat more complicated in nature, but seem to be equally at the mercy of the vagaries of this world. If anything happens to the electric power, we suddenly discover that air conditioners, refrigerators, and furnaces cease to operate. Taxes, together with an increase in the cost of gasoline, can impose severe restrictions on use of an automobile. The supermarket, where I can buy almost anything I may want, is a great convenience, except for those times when the supermarket happens to be closed by a strike. Banks are wonderful but my generation is still a little sensitive to thoughts of 1933 when the banks were closed. My church provides a generous pension, and yet facing the fact that it will need some supplement, I am confronted with the unfortunate information that the dollar I now put away toward an annuity is going to be worth only a half or a third as much by the time I get ready to use it. I may buy a 1961 model of some automobile of which I approve, and yet by the time 1961 comes around, I will discover that this definitive ultimate model, beyond which there could not be any possible improvement, has now decreased extraordinarily in value, and I am really driving a hopelessly antiquated and quite unsatisfactory machine. Advertisers then recommend that I invest, wisely and immediately, in a 1962 model.

Quite apart from the absurdity of laying aside for myself all these treasures that can disintegrate right before my eyes, there is the plain wrongness of putting my whole life's interest into things which I can control and own, and if I am so moved, distribute. All of it is at very best a partial use, but only in terms of the things which really matter, and the things which really matter are not treasures such as these.

We must of course face the fact that in our day there's another whole series of treasures, or at least values, which have come very much to the forefront. These values have to do with prestige and all that goes with it. It is probably only natural that most of us should wish to have the people of whom we are fond approve of us. We all like to think that we work surrounded by the good will and confidence of our friends. But when we begin to assume that the good will of our friends is directly commensurate with the importance of the position we hold or the honors we have received or the manner in which we live, we have suddenly arrived at a point of delusion which makes it almost impossible for friends to like us for any of the right reasons.

Our parents were raised on the strict theory that one should never explain. One's friends did not require it, and one's enemies would not believe it. The same kind of thinking might well apply to this whole matter of the values we call status. Professional people may well be required to live under certain rules governing exterior behavior and dress. This, for example, is true of the armed forces. To some degree it is true of the academic world, and it is certainly true in the Church. For obvious reasons, some businesses prefer to have their men dress in a conservative fashion and behave in a particular way. All of this is quite understandable. But this is not what I mean by status.

What I mean by status is rather the absurd notion that "art stopped short in the cultivated court of the Empress Josephine," or the equally absurd conviction that "art's immaculate conception was the Spanish Insurrection,"— when taken as a value judgment on oneself or on one's friends. The type of conformity which takes the world's mercurial standards as real is, of course, conformity to something so second-rate that the first-rate things of life have almost no chance of surviving.

These are different kinds of treasures, but they, too, are not permanent, and not really worth devoting one's life to. It was noted long ago that a good name can be stolen just as easily as a purse, but we should recognize always that there is some distinction between a good name and a public reputation for enjoying the right things and nothing else. The latter form of treasure can be swept away just as easily by the next change in the standards of the world's tastes.

"If you can't lick 'em, join 'em" is the somewhat cynical phrase dear to Americans when they are discussing political maneuvering. On the other hand, in American social history the exact reverse of the phrase has proved equally true. In either form, however, it is the negative aspect of a basic and enduring principle—if you wish to enlist a man's interest, give him a job; if you wish to gain his devotion, then let him contribute.

From the Middle Ages on it has been common knowledge that to aid a human being was to acquire an obligation. All of this is summed up more adequately in the phrase: *"Where your treasure is, there will your heart be also."* A proprietary interest is always a continuing one, and always has been. This is the basis of all nationalism, good or bad, and the root of all pride, good or bad. Taken as a statement apart from context, it is undeniably true, but at the same time is open to what Christians must call a "worldly" interpretation.

The context for this phrase is "treasure in heaven," not "treasure on earth." If we lay up for ourselves heavenly treasure, then our only concern will be a single-minded devotion to the riches which that phrase implies. Just what are these treasures? Certainly any list of them would have to include knowledge of the love of God, an appreciation of the love of friends, and a profound joy in the sharing of the gifts entrusted to one's care. The responsibility of the American conscience will readily convince people of the obligation of sharing their tremendous physical wealth, and no one remotely argues that this should not be done; but somehow this wealth only partakes of the nature of reality insofar as it is expressive of the sharing of much more enduring riches. The Apostles did not have silver and gold; but they shared Christ's health with the sick man and healed him. As citizens with world-wide responsibilities, we hear much in our day of the necessity of sharing our wealth with the other peoples of the world; but thoughtful men have been pointing out continuously that we are not sharing the one real treasure we have as a nation—our sense of responsible freedom under God. If this is our one great gift, then we had better be certain that this is as true of us individually as it is collectively. I must stop and consider occasionally what it is I really want most in the world.

In common with most of my generation, I have been brought up on the numberless variations of things people want at the particular ages at which they want them. The young want great opportunities; the mature want great responsibilities; the middle-aged want great wealth; but the aged will settle for a good digestion. There is, of course, nothing wrong with any one of these ambitions, provided they are thought through in terms of service, but it is tragically apparent that each is a disappointment if sought solely for its own sake. Opportunity can mean the acceptance of a difficult vocation; responsibility can mean the loneliness and misunderstanding which so often go with strict integrity. Great wealth can mean the encouragement of genius and the adjustment of some of the world's inequities. A good digestion can mean the quietness essential to first-class thinking in first-class men.

But these same things can damn a man. Opportunity, apart from God, can mean a hedgehopping, self-seeking opportunism which will help a man to rise by stepping upon the heads of others. Responsibility, not under God, can mean that consuming lust for power which can result in disappointing the souls and bodies of millions. Great wealth, apart from the sense of stewardship, can mean selfishness compounded to the point of neurosis or outright insanity. A good digestion, apart from its usefulness in terms of quiet thought, can be the sole ambition of a sluggish gourmand who wishes to sleep with quietness after one meal, only that he may be the better prepared to enjoy the next meal—a process which may be highly useful in raising hogs for the pork market, but is certainly less than an honest picture of a man.

My aims and desires necessarily change with my age, but I would be dishonest did I not concede frankly that if they are for anything short of the service of God and man, they will ruin me rather than satisfy me. It is only too clear that a grown man is the exact picture of the things he wants or desires. If my wants and desires are not of heaven, then they are of the earth; and if they are of the earth, then I am earth-bound. If I am earth-bound, then in Jesus' terms, I am an existing thing, but woefully short of being a living soul.

Thirteen

The light of the body is the eye: if therefore thine eye be single, thy whole body shall be full of light.

But if thine eye be evil, thy whole body shall be full of darkness. If therefore the light that is in thee be darkness, how great is that darkness!

No man can serve two masters: for either he will hate the one, and love the other; or else he will hold to the one, and despise the other. Ye cannot serve God and mammon.

Despite the fact that most confidence men are famous for their ability to look one straight in the eye, nearly all of us are convinced that we can learn almost all there is to know about people in following such a process. Any preacher learns fairly soon in life that his people would much rather have him look at and talk to them directly than have him read a sermon to them, no matter how excellently constructed the sermon might be. Our language, for instance, is colored with phrases which make it clear that the eye is regarded as expressive of the interior man:

bright-eyed, eagle-eyed, hawk-eyed, "The man came in with fire in his eye"—"He gazed with a sorrowful eye"—"Her eyes danced with pleasure"—or that almost liturgical phrase, "The eyes of Texas."

It is characteristic of our Lord that he takes this popular notion but exactly reverses its application. All of these phrases and their connotations have to do with showing what the eye reveals as going on inside of a man. As Jesus uses the illustration, the eye is the gate through which light comes from the outside into the man.

Nowadays we know a great deal about the exact proportion of impression taken in through the eye, as against the other senses. It is staggeringly high. However Jesus was not using this metaphor in terms of the physical senses, but rather as a figure for all the ways in which we, as human beings, apprehend the mysteries of the life all around us. The problem is simply this: what do I really take in?—what do I apprehend?—what do I comprehend?

Most of us have been amused by the story of two psychiatrists meeting and saying "good morning" to each other, after which each spends the rest of the day wondering what the other meant by the expression. Most of us often do the same thing. The President will make an utterance, and one side or the other, or both, will calmly assume that he made the utterance out of political necessity; it rarely occurs to either side that he might well have been speaking from a pure sense of responsibility. An important ecclesiastic will ask for aid for people in some stricken part of the world, and our first tendency is to dismiss it either on the grounds that the area is filled with his

coreligionists, or that since the area is not filled with his
coreligionists, then he wishes it to be. Yet the chances are
he is acting solely on the basis of conscience, charity, and
common humanity. A father comes home from work, and
the children greet him with joy. But how often this normal
reaction is viewed with suspicion, since it can mean either
that Mother has primed them to behave well, since it is
the first of the month and the bills have been slightly high,
or Christmas is approaching and the children are just
making a shrewd investment.

These are extraordinarily homely illustrations, but at
least they point to the type of thing most of us do far too
often. Being ourselves people of mixed motives, our first
tendency is to suspect mixed motives in others. If this is a
constant and continuing process, then it can lead only to
that madness wherein a man can view others only as creatures made in his own image, which is one way of stating
the ultimate blasphemy.

What am I to take on? By that disciplined observation,
which Jesus terms the "single" eye, I should see the world
exactly as it is, and insofar as it is possible understand
what God wants for it. I am not permitted to gloss over
cruelty or wickedness or dishonesty or violence. To do that
would be to indulge in the same pursuit for which the
false prophets were condemned—to say "peace" where
there is no peace. But neither am I permitted to see these
ugly manifestations of fallen, self-seeking human nature
as permanent and irremediable. I am obligated to be completely honest about the remedy.

As a human, and therefore limited, being, I do not

really know enough to know what a perfect world would be like. All attempts in the past to picture such a world have visualized a world cured of only those particular evils which the viewer recognized. This is never good enough; for there are always things which we regard as evil, such as slavery, which did not bother many people a few centuries ago. The civilized world does not nowadays regard as likely an aggressive war started for the sole purpose of increasing a particular nation's imperial boundaries. Yet, this really did not bother many people in the eighteenth century, and apparently bothered none in the seventeenth. All of us in this country have come to respect the live-and-let-live policy defined more formally as religious liberty. Yet the free exercise of religion as such is a very late seventeenth-century product. Up to that time it was common to permit the free exercise of only one religion (or at best, two) per country. Now, no one approves of burning witches; but on a point such as this, it is always well to remember the wickedly sly suggestion of C. S. Lewis that the real reason we do not approve of burning witches is not that we do not approve of burning, but rather, that we do not believe in witches. And this last point raises a very serious problem. How do we set about changing the world without using the very methods which have made the world the sort of place that needs to be changed? Being cruel to the cruel is not a change of method—just a change of masters. Oppressing a particular oppression out of existence still leaves nothing but oppression. How can I look at these changes in the civilized world's temper and judge them for what they really are? I suspect I know how, but the answer has to include a whole lot of old-fashioned and un-popular words.

It means viewing changes in national sovereignty as the result of patriotism dictated by a firm conviction that God demands that his people be free. Of course, patriotism is not in our day regarded as an accepted or realistic word. It implies some kind of emotional response to a theory. That, of course, cannot be regarded as realistic in modern terms, although I have never quite been able to understand what was unrealistic about being shot, or hanged, or maimed, or starved out of devotion to an ideal.

In the gradually civilized treatment of prisoners and the insane I have to discern the quiet and granitelike concern of Quakers. In the abolition of the slave trade I have to remember that this was the fruit of evangelical Christianity. To view the abolition of slavery as due primarily to its lack of economic success, as against growing industrialism, is to forget some of the most inspired words ever said on the subject—words said by a Southerner in the Virginia Legislature years before there was any effective external pressure in the matter.

All of these are, in their own particular way, patriotic, since they derive from a love of God so great that it cannot accept the country at less than its best.

The second unpopular word is "charity." This word, which is the English Bible's translation of the word St. Paul uses to describe the passionate and utterly selfless love which God has for his people, has come to have a rather cold-blooded connotation. Charity is that for which we get a 10 per cent allowance on our income tax. It is no longer thought of as something we do for a person. But there really is no better word—and the problem is not really the word, it is what we have done to it.

In common with most important words, it is easier to say what charity is not than to say what it is. It is perfectly clear that it is not the giving of self-protective alms, nor is it a fixed smile in the face of human suffering. It is not organizing a committee to deal with human beings as though they were just sets of statistical data.

Charity is, rather, that passionate concern for the welfare of another, a concern which will not be put off by ingratitude or failure in obedience or even that most subtle quality of the Devil, the terrible suspicion that one is doing an act of kindness for a mixed motive.

Charity is admittedly the most difficult of the virtues in terms of actual practice, because the problem inevitably arises: how much can I do for somebody else without falling into that condescending frame of mind which will have me do things for another which he really ought to be learning to do for himself. It is charity in the stricter sense for me to take a little child's hand when a child wants to cross a busy intersection, but it ceases to be charity when, by force of personal or professional competence, I presume to lead grown people across the far more terrifying intersections of life.

Obviously, if a person asks my advice and really wants it, I am obligated to give it, but even then only in terms which charity permits. The best criterion is Jesus' own method. When people asked him for advice, he gave it;

but always on such terms that they who asked had to make up their own minds.

Who is my neighbor? The answer is an illustration of neighborliness which permits only one possible conclusion, but the man who asked the question had to draw the conclusion for himself.

Many of us can remember the insufferable humiliation of the dole: men wanting to work, but unable to find employment. This left a deep scar in the economy of our country that accounts for much of the seemingly intransigent attitude of certain unions when it comes to the problem of co-operating with the introduction of labor-saving devices and general mechanization which could easily damage the economic production of the country. It was indeed the dole that did more than anything else to give "charity" its bad connotation. In the sense of the dole, no self-respecting man wants to be an object of charity.

This is a tragic misunderstanding of the word, for in its real sense, no living human heart can exist unless it is the object of charity, God's and man's. True charity means that I am aware of my need for my friends. I cannot even be myself unless I find in them "other" beings infinitely and equally precious to God.

Jesus has changed the metaphor in this particular saying, and if we are not careful, we may miss his point. If we do not remember that the eye is the gate through which light enters, then we will not appreciate the point that we control that gate. Each person alive has some of the divine light in him, and the world, even in its grimmest moments, sheds some of the light of that charitable concern of God which we call "judgment." To shut the gate on the smallest portion of that light is to permit the internal darkness to take over, and "how great is that darkness!"

One cannot absorb both light and darkness at the same time. No person can, at one and the same time, serve two masters. The God of the universe, he whom Jesus calls "Father," operates on one set of standards; and the god whom worldly men tend to worship, that which Jesus calls "Mammon," operates on a totally different set of standards. God is concerned with the things which matter in all eternity, and Mammon is concerned totally with the quick profit made and taken—regardless of what it does to other human beings.

In the New Testament—apart from those passages touching on God's love for the world he created—the world in which we live and the Prince of that world, the Devil, are both regarded as enemies. It is the world that teaches little children the prejudices and antagonisms which make them grow up into people such as we. It is the wisdom of this world that changes the loving generosity of the young into the self-seeking hardness of the old. It is the Prince of this world who attaches the generous enthusiasm of youth to the persons and gangs which can well destroy them. It is Mammon which makes a man abandon to the state moral obligations that are his own. It is Mammon which is the authority of our cutthroat competition, all pitiless exploitation, all trampling on the hearts and souls and injuries to others done in aid of one's own alleged progress. It is Mammon which dictates, "You have to be tough in this world to get ahead"—a statement which is entirely true. If one accepts Mammon's definition of "getting ahead," it is only too easy to see that definition exemplified in the persons who have followed it. They will be powerful men, that is to say, they will be in a position to hurt a number of people. They will be arrogant men, because their habitual beating down of others will have left them with the false conclusion that they are somehow superior. They will be rich men, according to their own definition of riches; but they will also be inexpressively lonely men, gnawed by the endless fear of the loss of the only thing which gives them importance. They will be frustrated men, miserable and insecure in the midst of all which they thought the world had to offer. In the terms of the New Testament, which saw this world to be synonymous with sickness and hell, a living death, these men only managed to make their hell right here a little more hellish. It is a curious definition of "getting ahead."

Mammon, to the Hebrew, meant riches as this world considers them. This world considers them to be things which we make, which we control, and which are ours; whereas the children of the Kingdom regard the riches of the good earth as things which God makes, which God controls, and which are, at the very most, only entrusted to our care.

I have sometimes heard numbers of would-be rich men complain of the seeming injustices of the New Testament. (Even admitting that Joseph of Arimathea, a rich man, comes in for praise, the New Testament in general, and Jesus in particular, seems harsh toward the rich.) But I have never known any really rich man to quarrel with Jesus' phrase, *a rich man shall hardly enter into the kingdom of heaven.* The really rich know only too well the dangers that beset them. No one is more conscious than they of the difficulty of being sure friends are friendly for totally disinterested reasons.

But "rich" in this sense is not really the problem at all. The problem is, as it always was, that of a false standard of values. To try to maintain both standards will result only in a spiritual form of schizophrenia which is, in some ways, more terrible than the ordinary form, for this one permits no happy interludes of escape.

Fourteen

Therefore I say unto you, Take no thought for your life, what ye shall eat, or what ye shall drink; nor yet for your body, what ye shall put on. Is not the life more than meat, and the body more than raiment?

Behold the fowls of the air: for they sow not, neither do they reap, nor gather into barns; yet your heavenly Father feedeth them. Are ye not much better than they?

Which of you by taking thought can add one cubit unto his stature?

And why take ye thought for raiment? Consider the lilies of the field, how they grow; they toil not, neither do they spin:

And yet I say unto you, That even Solomon in all his glory was not arrayed like one of these.

Wherefore, if God so clothe the grass of the field, which to day is, and to morrow is cast into the oven, shall he not much more clothe you, O ye of little faith?

Therefore take no thought, saying, What shall we eat?

or, What shall we drink? or, Wherewithal shall we be clothed?

(For after all these things do the Gentiles seek:) for your heavenly Father knoweth that ye have need of all these things.

But seek ye first the kingdom of God, and his righteousness; and all these things shall be added unto you.

Take therefore no thought for the morrow: for the morrow shall take thought for the things of itself. Sufficient unto the day is the evil thereof.

Jesus has no patience with anxious thought, what we know in modern terms as anxiety or worry. That a man has to be fed and clothed is no news to God. The problem is never "Where shall I get clothing?" but "What job shall I do?" In a world controlled by God, men can always be clothed in whatever clothing is necessary for the performance of the work God gives them to do. In peaceful times food will always be provided for those who work hard. In troubled times one may have to suffer; but one never suffers alone, nor does a godly man ever suffer without serving some godly purpose. Whatever is necessary for the purpose will be given.

The real difficulty is that men who mind earthly things frequently have false standards, and the human tendency is not to pray for daily bread, but to pray for a particular kind of bread; not to ask humbly that God will clothe us for whatever task he gives us, but that he will clothe us in a certain kind of clothing. To be anxious about lesser things inevitably means the neglect of greater things. And the greater things are the things of the Kingdom—the things which go with our humble daily service of our God. It sounds fatuous to observe that existence exists, but that is exactly the point.

In the natural order, man can always feed himself; but his worry about delicacies in place of the simple things provided is to ignore the natural order. The birds do not consciously do any kind of work at all, and yet quite unconsciously they are responsible for spreading seeds of all sorts to all places of the world; they manage to get fed because their existence dictates it. Animals of the type which have to store up food do so, but if the weather remains mild and food plentiful, they never gorge themselves on their stored-up food. Only human beings do that.

Our souls are housed in bodies over whose appearance we have only relatively little control. I cannot, by thinking about it, make myself taller; nor could I, by worrying about it, grow a new head of hair. I can control the amount of flesh I accumulate on my bones, but even that ceases to be a problem, if I am profoundly occupied in work worth doing. A man engrossed in his work will often forget to eat, but he rarely seems to suffer from it. When it is really necessary for him to eat, nature will remind him.

A man with tremendous concerns may well do with very little sleep, but this will generally mean that he will get all the sleep he needs, even if it does come at odd times. Overwork, lack of sleep, and irregular eating habits only become serious problems when a man faces the fact that he is laboring on a job not worth doing, or when he realizes that he is not doing well the job he has to do, or when he becomes convinced that he is not being recognized or rewarded in proportion to his labors. These are all roots of anxiety, and it is anxiety which breaks men down, not lack of food, sleep, or money.

As to clothing, the average man is in wintertime spared the competitive custom of modern dressing. In the summer however and especially at the beach, he seems to be gradually reasserting that more spectacular plumage which characterizes the males of a theoretically less useful species. As a man I am, of course, not competent to make any observations about women's clothing, but in my obscure way, I gather from popular advertising that the point of Jesus' observation is still pertinent. There is just too much worrying about decking oneself out—not warmth, but mink; not cloth, but the finest woolen; not a signet ring, but a sapphire. There is of course nothing intrinsically wrong with colorful and handsome clothing. Indeed, there is much to be said for what a new, wild hat will do for a woman's whole inner being; but to give one's whole attention to such things is obviously some form of perversion. For richness and beauty a field of anemones is always going to come off better than any individual person, no matter how richly dressed. Again the problem is not the clothing. The problem is worrying about it. The Gospel illustration is rather pointed. Jesus did not choose for an example the king most admired for his honesty, or the one most admired for his bravery. Rather, he chose the one commemorated in Israel by his worldly wisdom and the splendor of his external trappings. There is just the slightest hint that Solomon had almost nothing to glory in except his clothes; and yet Solomon with all this glory was not as wonderful to behold as a field of anemones. The anemones have a momentary beauty, and yet, as soon as they have dried, their beauty is gone and they, too, serve only the practical purpose of providing fuel for a peasant oven.

Surely the immortal soul of man is to be clothed in something more permanent than that. Think back to the suit for which you spent too much money twenty-five years ago. Think back to the dress which was so important that you, as a young girl, would be ruined forever if you did not have it. Where is either that suit or that dress right now?

The chances are that the only clothing you own which is twenty-five or more years old will be an austere, lovingly made white dress worn by the baby of your family at baptism. If you are a woman, you may well have your own and your mother's wedding dress. But what made you keep either? It was not their richness nor their beauty, but instead, that permanent good thing with which they have been associated. The clothes that matter, even for us, seem to be only those which are necessary for the work of the Kingdom.

It will be observed that any literal understanding of Jesus' words would end up by doing away with both savings and life insurance. The term "life insurance" is of course rather misleading; no company on earth can insure anybody that he will continue to live. All it insures is the proper handling of a man's moral responsibilities after he has died. There is not the slightest assurance that a savings account will inevitably benefit the person doing the saving. Probably the exact distinction between thrift and avarice, between the responsible man and the miser, is the frank recognition that one saves only in terms of responsibility, never in terms of greed.

To eat all which one can afford to eat will be, for most American people, nothing but gormandizing. To drink all one can afford to drink may produce nothing but drunkenness. To spend all which one has is done, more often than not, on the immoral assumption that someone else will then take over and foot the bills. To sleep as long as one can sleep; to dream as long as one can dream; to work until one drops—all are equally irresponsible acts, irresponsible to the point of being sinful. The discipline which dictates the forgoing of an immediate pleasure for the sake of a future responsibility is the very first lesson to be learned from any competent school of ethics. This forgoing, this discipline, is good for the sake of the training gained by it. Indeed, it should be remembered that our word "ascetic," which so often conjures up for us the picture of a stern, restrained spiritual giant, is actually the Greek word for "athlete." Athletes have to be trained under discipline so that when their strength and endurance are required, they have the stamina to perform satisfactorily.

I may not live another day, but even if I do not, I will be a better man for the remainder of this day for having disciplined my time, my strength, my energy, and my income—all things which I can call mine only by common custom. Actually, all of them were lent to me, and I am responsible to my God for each one of them. If I deprive myself in Lent in order to have extra money to give away, that is a worthy thing. If I deprive myself in Lent only that

I may gorge myself after Easter, I am guilty of nothing other than a compound sin, the most perverted form of sensuality.

If I put money aside now—money which is ultimately God's gift—for the purpose of insuring that my responsibilities are met when I am old, or even if I were to die right now, I am still trying to take care of the responsibilities which God has laid on me, with the understanding that they, too, are ultimately God's gift. If, on the other hand, I save and scrounge and starve in order to have a vast sum of money when I am old, neglecting in the meantime the responsibilities and concerns which God lays on me, I shall be left when I am old with only one thing—the inescapable habit of saving, scrounging, and starving. The miser is one of the world's most tragic figures. The real point, of course, is that we must avoid the gnawing, faithless, and consuming worry which always causes us to neglect the good things of the day for fear that the morrow may be less pleasant; or, indeed, to take the cares and troubles of the day as though they were definitive, and the morrow could bring inevitably nothing but something worse.

We miss much of the point if we do not observe the gentle smile on Jesus' face when he says, Don't worry about tomorrow. Tomorrow is another day with its own set of joys, cares, and problems. You have troubles enough for the one day you really know anything about, today, so why not concentrate on that?

Fifteen

Judge not, that ye be not judged.

For with what judgment ye judge, ye shall be judged: and with what measure ye mete, it shall be measured to you again.

And why beholdest thou the mote that is in thy brother's eye, but considerest not the beam that is in thine own eye?

Or how wilt thou say to thy brother, Let me pull out the mote out of thine eye; and, behold, a beam is in thine own eye?

Thou hypocrite, first cast out the beam out of thine own eye; and then shalt thou see clearly to cast out the mote out of thy brother's eye.

The cold irony which Jesus manifests in his whole handling of judgment is even colder and more ironic than it seems at first reading. The figure is this: a man with a two-by-four sticking out of his own eye is critically concerned over the speck of sawdust that is in his brother's eye; he is so concerned that he cannot rest until he has removed the speck. Obviously with this timber sticking out of his own eye he cannot see clearly to remove a speck from his brother's eye; but there is a further and terrible implication. The exterior of the human eye reflects the image which it is, at the same time, absorbing, so there is the dread possibility that the speck is not really there at all. It is nothing other than a reflection of the beam in one's own eye.

Judgment belongs to God alone, and even God's Son will refuse to be a judge, or be a divider over men. Judgment is a curious faculty of the human mind. We pray to have right judgment in all things, but by the time we finish the New Testament, this particular usage of the word is so apart from the world's use of it as to be talking about something totally different. "Right judgment" means "the faculty of concluding a thought process with affirmation or denial"; whereas "judgment," as we commonly use it, means "the faculty of affirming or denying a conclusion based on a direct comparison of objects, or ideas, or persons."

"Judgment," as we use it, means the sort of thing I do when I look at my brother and say I am better than he. It is the sort of thing which will permit an unhappily married woman to be violently condemnatory of some woman who got a divorce. Any psychologist or psychiatrist will assure us that the things we tend to be most bitter about in the actions of others are the very things which we ourselves are most tempted to do. One of my colleagues recently told me of a fascinating test given by a psychiatrist to a group of seminarians. Each man was asked to describe the clergyman he most venerated and admired; then to describe the clergyman for whom he had tremendous respect, but no affection; and lastly to describe the clergyman who was so reprehensible he could not possibly stand him. At the conclusion of the test, without much being said, most of the men were shrewd enough to discover that all they had done was to describe three sides of their own individual characters.

A man working for a great firm will notice that one of his acquaintances in the same firm is not only consumed by ambition, but is ruthless in pursuing his objectives. To view the matter honestly, we would probably have to agree that the man who bitterly resents the situation is a man with similar objectives who is so ambitious as to be hurt by the ruthlessness. He may well have moral restraints which do not permit him to be equally ruthless, but it is just as certain that his real conflict lies in the fact that he and the other man are rivals for the same job.

Gossip is one of the Devil's ways of spreading false comparisons for the purpose of making judgments. So-and-so is an alcoholic, which means clearly, of course, that he has no moral stamina, no will power, no integrity, and no care for his family or friends. This is one of the easy generalizations which are current in this country all the time. Let us think a moment about this man. In the first place, he may have put up battle after battle, the courage and tenacity of which might well beggar what I would think of as my strongest effort in life. In this instance it is wise to remember that persistent attitude of the British— a war is only won in the last battle. We assume that this man has no moral stamina, or care for his family. Any good physician asked to treat this alcoholic would, first of all, want to know what it was that made him drink. What desperate unhappiness or frustration caused him to seek this false support or form of escape. The chances are that his alcoholism exists because he does have morals. Had he no morals, there would be no conflict. It may be that he feels unequal to his job. It may be that he is still loyal to a wife who has ceased to love him. It may be that he and his children are so far apart they can no longer talk to each other. It may be that he is in love with some other woman, and basic decency and morality will not let him hurt his wife. All these and countless other reasons may explain the man's deplorable habit.

Ultimately it is only God who knows; and therefore it is only God who can judge. Our pictures are only partial pictures, and as partial pictures they fall short of the truth, for the truth must be the whole picture—as only God can see it.

It is extremely easy at the moment to enlist public interest on the subject of the general reaction of honesty, which came to light a few months ago in the public scandal over quiz programs. Strong editorials were carried in most newspapers, some quite objective and some carried away by sentimentality. Either point of view is understandable, whether one agrees or not. The disappointing feature of it all was the bitter attack on individual human beings publicly put under severe and seemingly final judgments. These judgments were all the more vindictive because some of the individuals had, as participants, enjoyed the equally unthinking admiration of millions of their fellow citizens.

However "moral" this may be as a reaction, it is certainly not the reaction of Jesus.

None was more coldly nor witheringly condemning of sin than he; and yet he could always manage to separate the sin from the sinner. He could castigate the lawyers of his day, and at the same time show gentle concern with an individual lawyer. He had little regard for the rulers as a class; and yet it was the inability of one rich young ruler to recognize his true vocation which moved Jesus so deeply that the Gospeler took pains to record it.

No one remotely questions the horror of the shock of sin. Saul of Tarsus quite frankly presided at the martyrdom of St. Stephen: this was a sinful, wicked act. But it is simply impossible to calculate the Church's loss had it so confused Saul with his sin that it could have forever prevented the repented and converted Saul from becoming St. Paul. The calendar of saints is full of the names of violent and bloody men who, through one means or another, came to be God's friends; but the calendar also contains the names of such men as St. Augustine, who never really committed any crimes for which society at large in their own day would have condemned them. St. Augustine, in the days of his sin, really did not do anything which the world would have judged wrong. He was just living a kind of life that he would have to change were he ever to take his mother's religion seriously. He changed. We must not, however, forget the fact that he was loved into Christianity, not bullied into it. His mother and his few Christian friends did not, by their judging attitude, frighten away this passionate man; rather, following the example of their Lord, they just insisted on continuing to see him in terms of what he could be instead of in terms of what he was.

Another famous illustration of the Christian attitude is that of St. Ambrose forbidding the emperor entrance to the cathedral because of the wholesale slaughter in which the imperial troops had, on the emperor's order, indulged themselves in punishing a rebellious city. Here was sin in a big way—that which in the quaint language of the six-teenth century was called "open and notorious evil" living. But Ambrose's attitude was such that the emperor re-pented. Ambrose had that gift of great spiritual leaders, the ability to show a man the dreadful results of his actions in such a way that the man himself was all the time deeply conscious of his counselor's love.

There is, however, another whole field of judgment which is of deep concern to most people, and that is the judgment of oneself. Modern psychiatry has but docu-mented St. Paul's intuitive insight into this matter of self-judgment. In his first great Letter to the Corinthians (as J. B. Phillips translates it) St. Paul includes this important passage:

"You should look upon us as ministers of Christ, as trustees of the secrets of God. And it is a prime requisite in a trustee that he should prove worthy of his trust. But, as a matter of fact, it matters very little to me what you, or any man, thinks of me—I don't even value my opinion of myself. For I might be quite ignorant of any fault in myself—but that doesn't justify me before God. My only true judge is God himself.

"The moral of this is that we should make no hasty or

premature judgments. When the Lord comes he will bring into the light of day all that at present is hidden in darkness, and he will expose the secret motives of men's hearts. Then shall God himself give each man his share of praise."

It is the writing of an honest and very humble soul. St. Paul was fully aware of the things which he could do well; but he learned the hard way that God was more effective through him in the things which he did not do well. Surrounding his great gifts was the armor plate of self-confidence, just as most of us have internal areas which we do not make the subject of prayer because we are really quite convinced that these areas are completely godly, and do not require help from anybody. But these areas which St. Paul recognized as his "weaknesses," the things about which he prayed constantly, turned out ultimately to be the vehicles of God's strength. St. Paul's own account of it is deeply moving. He has just written of the splendor of his own spiritual experiences, and then goes on to say:

Of such an one will I glory: yet of myself I will not glory, but in mine infirmities.

For though I would desire to glory, I shall not be a fool; for I will say the truth: but now I forbear, lest any man should think of me above that which he seeth me to be, or that he heareth of me.

And lest I should be exalted above measure through the abundance of the revelations, there was given to me a thorn in the flesh, the messenger of Satan to buffet me, lest I should be exalted above measure.

For this thing I besought the Lord thrice, that it might depart from me.

*And he said unto me, My grace is sufficient for thee:
for my strength is made perfect in weakness. Most gladly
therefore will I rather glory in my infirmities, that the
power of Christ may rest upon me.*

St. Paul speaks to men in every age because of his transparent honesty. We, just as he, often do things we do not
understand. Often we do not do the things we really want
to do, and far too often we do the things we do not want
to do because each of us is an individual combination of
heredity, environment, brain, and appetite subject to the
ruling drive of the spirit of God. It is only this overruling
drive which makes a man unhappy about the sort of being
he is. But Jesus would have a man remember that even
judgment on oneself is an incomplete picture, because what
it really means is that one part of a man is judging another part of the same man—whether the judgment be
right or wrong, it can at best be but partial, and if it is less
than the whole picture, it is not true.

Without standards neither man nor his society could survive; but the Christian's job is to maintain these standards
—that which the Church calls "right judgment in all
things"—and to avoid those ultimate condemnations of
human beings which the church would term "wrong judgment in all things." Whether it be a beam or a mote,
neither can be removed save in love.

Probably one of the most profound observations ever
made was this simple advice: whether it be the worship of
God or the love of your neighbor, the most important thing
for us to do is to get out of God's way.

Sixteen

Give not that which is holy unto the dogs, neither cast ye your pearls before swine, lest they trample them under their feet, and turn again and rend you.

The poetic form of this particular passage often means that it makes no sense to people who are not used to its XY, YX construction. What it is actually saying is this: "Give not that which is holy unto the dogs, lest they turn and rend you; neither cast ye your pearls before swine, lest they trample them under their feet." The sense of the words being understandable, we must be certain that we take Jesus seriously in this whole matter to which he refers: that of conveying religious truth. Most of us can remember in school or in college hearing sets of blasphemous words sung to hymn tunes. There is even one very pointless stanza dear to the army which is sung over and over again to the tune of "Onward Christian Soldiers," the entire text being "Lloyd George knew my father; father knew Lloyd George." None of this of course is seriously intentioned, and while some of the college versions may raise a serious problem as to taste, the context is such that they do no lasting damage.

There is another level, a far more serious one; that is the context in which religious truth may honestly and effectively be expressed. Probably the constant, public sin of the clergy is the prayers that they say at the start of purely secular events. Grace before meals is always appropriate. Prayer before an important political action is certainly most appropriate. But the real difficulty is that most of the prayers said on such public occasions are not really prayers at all. They tend to be well or poorly done addresses to God, making clear the prejudices and ambitions of the people present and things already agreed on, and not in the slightest degree expressive of any desire for God's help in the matter.

But this is only one aspect of the problem as we meet it everyday. Another one is the unfortunate habit of hauling in some religious text to justify a secular end. If, in the midst of a speech on some highly debatable matter, a politician rings the chimes of religion to justify his side of the argument, the dogs which will turn and rend him will be the very facts themselves. I am not concerned that the politician might himself look ridiculous; rather, I am concerned that a passage of Scripture has become a source of amusement to a number of people. Surely this is the real danger—that the too easy handling of the truths of religion can have no effect but that of making religion itself seem trivial. I suppose it is the real meaning of the Commandment against taking God's name in vain. Word-mongering has always been a very tricky profession, and the ease with which the words of religion may be quoted out of context only serves to make them a fascinating lure for the thoughtless.

We should understand clearly that dogs and swine are perfectly useful creatures and Jesus in no wise intends to use them as examples of perversity and lack of appreciation. The point is that a dog's job is to be a dog, and to demand from a dog a reaction possible only from a human being is not only to be unfair to the dog, but to be unfair as well to the idea or object for which we are trying to evoke a human reaction.

Pigs are not interested in pearls, which does not mean that there is anything wrong either with pearls or pigs. It just means that the pearl which calls forth the admiration of human beings calls forth absolutely nothing from the pigs. Whether a pearl or a hammer, the pig would simply disregard it and trample it in the mire. This, Jesus teaches, is not only unfair to the pearl, it is also unfair to the pigs.

The illustration emphasizes the fact that the truth by which we live is truth within a context. It does not seem necessary to go to the point of some of the ancient fathers in interpreting that dogs and swine really stand for Samaritans and Gentiles. Indeed, as I understand it, the illustration applied with equal validity to Israel itself.

The Epistle to the Hebrews uses a different illustration, but the point is just the same when it insists that strong meat is for grown men, but milk is for babies.

Over and over again a young man will come to a seminary filled with a staggering amount of misinformation, having definitive answers to certain problems to which God has not given any answer, and completely unaware of the more awesome and ultimate problems which lie at the heart of true religion. Often these men have a very difficult time coming to terms with facts and genuinely scholarly learning. Often there is a serious period of re-adjustment as they start to base their religion on the ancient rock of the Apostolic Confession, as they learn to become more childlike and grow in wisdom. But remember—these men are studying at a graduate level. They have already been through some of the best colleges and universities in the country; most of them have taken brilliant degrees; they are men who, with equal ease, could excel in half a dozen other learned vocations. If it is difficult for them, think what it would be like to expose some really very simple person to this same treatment.

Unfortunately, we know only too well that the failure to communicate is often so great that some very earnest people in every Christian Communion wonder whether their clergy are themselves really believing Christians. It is doubtless a great failing on my part, but I am unable to see many advantages of shock treatment in preaching. That human beings should be stirred from their lethargy is inevitable if the Word of God shall be preached. That it is desperately important that great minds in other fields should be fully aware of the Church's most mature thought is essential. But I simply do not understand what is to be gained when an ordinary sermon raises highly technical problems of a textual criticism when the basic preaching point remains just the same. Too often, for example, the point of one of the best books in the Old Testament is entirely lost to the layman because all he can remember is whether the preacher did or did not believe that Jonah was swallowed by a whale.

It is, of course, essential that our clergy be well educated and that they know how the Church and the Scriptures got to be the way they are. But it is equally important that the clergy remember the simple directness of Jesus, who could handle a most complicated point in such a way that a child made sense out of it and a saint was lost in wonder at its depth and implication. This, however, is a problem for the clergy.

What about the layman in his handling of religion? Pious prayer cards left in commercial offices have not as yet done any really noble service to religion. Prayer groups in parishes have often given unprepared people nothing but a sense of unreality. An open Bible on an executive's desk may produce little besides a somewhat justifiable doubt as to how busy he is or how sound his secular judgment may be. Certainly executives ought to pray and ought to be using their Bibles. But the evidence of the prayer and the Bible reading should show in attitude, not in things—things which may well lead another, rightly or wrongly, to suspect that they are only props. There is again the even more serious matter of sharing religious experience. In my Communion, when a man applies for Holy Orders, he has to state his reasons. But the simple, practical wisdom of life very rarely dictates that he state the complete list of his reasons, assuming that he knows them.

My colleagues and I often wonder how the authorities would react were they to receive a letter from a man who said that his vocation had come by a direct vision of the Lord, who thought he probably left his body and had a vision of heaven, who insisted he was right and therefore that almost everybody else was wrong, and who, on the whole, did not like women. Fortunately St. Paul did not have to write one, at least to the authorities. I suspect that a man writing such a letter could convince his bishop of both his vocation and his sanity, but under almost no possible circumstances could he hope to make such a thing intelligible to a committee. This does not mean that he could not do it with individual members of the committee. It just means that the committee as a whole is not the proper context for such revelation.

A man or woman will often regret disclosure of some intimate human reaction; the same thing is true of the disclosure of religious experience. In a burst of enthusiasm at some group meeting, a person will, with complete honesty and good will, mention some intimate religious detail of his life, only to learn a week or so later that this tale has become a matter of gossip or a basis for criticism. Intimate relations between persons are not easily shared, and religion is an intimate relationship between persons. You can safely share your relationship with God only with another person who is bound into the same relationship—that simplest definition of the Church, "two or three people gathered together in Jesus' name and completely agreed upon a matter." Christian sanctity is best served by feeding God's creatures that which by nature they were designed to eat, rather than by entrusting to them valuable objects which they by nature are not designed to value. This is on the whole a very harsh saying, but it is the harshness of honesty subject to love.

Earlier I mentioned Jonah, and for anyone who will take religion seriously, it is well to get to know him better. He is a most satisfactory man, sufficiently cranky and world-weary to make most of us feel completely at home with him. Consider the picture. God tells Jonah to go to the people of Nineveh and tell them that they are "in for it," that God is fed up with them, and that he will no longer tolerate them on the face of the earth. Jonah couldn't be less impressed. "I know what you're like. If I go and do as you say, you'll let me down; you always do, you're not to be trusted."

After the meditation, Jonah sets off in the opposite direction. The ship he is on is promptly met by a terrible storm. The sailors figure out that it is Jonah at whom the Lord is furious, so they dump him overboard. This is no solution, for the Lord has a great fish all ready to transport Jonah to dry land whence he can go on the journey God had commanded.

The second time Jonah is told to go to Nineveh and cry against it he does it and, sure enough, just as soon as he promises inevitable destruction, the wretched people repent in sackcloth and ashes. The Lord changes his mind. Jonah is livid. "Wasn't this just what I said you'd do? You're so softhearted and kindly you can't stay mad, and consequently you always change your mind. Just let's not bother any longer; let me die and I'll be a lot better off."

The Lord merely says, "You're pretty angry, aren't you?" Jonah goes out to the outskirts of the city, and builds himself a lean-to so that he can sulk in comfort, and see what happens. God causes a swift-growing bush to grow up beside Jonah's lean-to, and give him some real shelter. Jonah is for the first time actually happy about life.

Next, God prepares a worm to destroy the bush. (What a religion it is which can imagine the Mind behind the Universe preparing a worm!) The bush withers, God sends the terrible east wind and nearly kills Jonah with heat and misery. Jonah now really wishes he were dead. God now says, "I suppose you think you have a right to be angry about the bush?"

Jonah replies, "I certainly do; I'm so mad I could die!"

The ending is so splendid I shall not presume to paraphrase it in my breezy style.

Then said the Lord, Thou has had pity on the gourd, for the which thou hast not laboured, neither madest it grow; which came up in a night, and perished in a night:

And should not I spare Nineveh, that great city, wherein are more than sixscore thousand persons that cannot discern between their right hand and their left hand; and also much cattle?

Those of us who have wrestled with God understand only too well Jonah's reactions. Like Jacob, however, we have learned that wrestling with God always leaves us lame, defeated, exhausted—and infinitely satisfied. Whether it be Jacob, Jonah, or Don Camillo, there is the inevitable sense of God's needling us out of love and in the interests of aims above and beyond human judgment, human patience, and the human heart.

I confess to having spent half my life being outraged and concerned over human difficulties, and wishing that something could be done about them, only to discover that the somebody called to do something about them was the tired, outraged, concerned man doing the praying: myself.

Seventeen

Ask, and it shall be given you; seek, and ye shall find; knock, and it shall be opened unto you:

For every one that asketh receiveth; and he that seeketh findeth; and to him that knocketh it shall be opened.

Or what man is there of you, whom if his son ask bread, will he give him a stone?

Or if he ask a fish, will he give him a serpent?

If ye then, being evil, know how to give good gifts unto your children, how much more shall your Father which is in heaven give good things to them that ask him?

Therefore all things whatsoever ye would that men should do to you, do ye even so to them: for this is the law and the prophets.

Jesus in all his teaching starts with the known and moves to the unknown; on the familiar peg he hangs the cloak of greater understanding. In the text under consideration, he makes use of one of the most familiar but also most intimate and demanding relationships in the world: that between parent and child.

The crowd in front of Jesus was just a crowd as you and I know. It was made up of people such as we know: some of them were very good, some very bad, but most of them neither very good nor very bad. And yet, not even the worst of us will fail to respond to the needs of our own children, though we may not be largehearted enough to do anything for anybody else's children. This is the known; this is the recognizable. If a son ask his father for bread, would he give him a stone? (Remember that the yellow oval stones of Palestine looked just like the local bread.) If the boy asked for a fish, would he give him a serpent? After all, a serpent and an eel to a small boy look just alike, but one can feed him, the other can kill him.

St. Luke quotes Jesus as asking an additional question, one which St. Matthew omits. It is this: If the boy asks for an egg, will the father give him a scorpion, a creature which when all curled up looks exactly like an egg? The exception is not important because the basic point is the same. Ordinary, sinful human beings will be good to their own children. How much more will the Father in Heaven, who is not ordinary and is not sinful and is not mortal, give good things to all of his children who ask him?

What is God like? God is like the best human father, only ever so much more. Our approach to God, then, needs only to be childlike. Jesus says, *Ask, and it shall be given you; seek, and ye shall find; knock, and it shall be open unto you.*

Surely this invitation is a little too all-inclusive. It certainly cannot mean that I can ask anything I want and then expect to have it. As St. James pointed out, *"Ye ask, and receive not, because ye ask amiss, that ye may consume it upon your lusts."* The word "lust" means "a strong, passionate, or inordinate desire." In this definition it is rather important to remember that the adjective "inordinate" means "not restricted or restrained by prescribed rules or bounds, or questions of right or reason." In everyday language, we generally use the word "lust" almost exclusively of inordinate desire for sexual satisfaction. This is a secondary, derived meaning; we are dealing in this context with the first one.

What may I ask? I may ask anything which is for the common welfare of all of God's children. I may ask for anything which will enable me better to serve my brothers. I may not ask for something which I can only have at somebody else's expense. I may not ask for anything which is only going to serve to magnify my own position. In practical terms, what does this mean? It means I may ask God for money to buy up the tax liens on the house of an aged parishioner. (In modern social economy, you will remember, the only helpless people are those not quite poverty-stricken who still try to pay their own bills.) As a young clergyman I did just this. I prayed with a passionate intensity in this matter. God did not create a special set of treasury notes to meet the need, but what he did do was to move the heart of one very nominal member of my parish to send me, for no particular reason and totally subject to my discretion, a check which was just five dollars short of the sum I needed.

It also means that I may ask God for the sheer physical strength to carry on an impossible job when the job is worth doing for the sake of his other children. It is fairly easy to tell whether such strength is God's gift, or just the product of nervous and emotional excitement. If it is God's gift, then at the conclusion of the whole crisis one is not particularly aware of cumulative fatigue. If it is just nervous and emotional energy, as soon as the crisis is passed, a most terrible letdown will occur. I suspect this is why aged and wise physicians can go on endlessly without suffering any ill effects.

Our Lord's words also mean that I may pray that so-and-so will become a Christian—but not a Christian at somebody else's expense. St. Gregory of Nyssa observed many centuries ago that the proper pilgrimage for a monk was to go from earth to heaven, not from Byzantium to Jerusalem. It is important we remember this when we are praying about the conversion of people. According to the New Testament, it is quite in order to desire the office of bishop, but only provided one wants to do good work—a work to which one is called by the Body of Christ. Therefore, while I can readily understand the Church praying with intensity over the choice of a bishop, I do not remotely understand a man praying with intensity to be one. Indeed, the man can probably only desire the office after he has been called to it, and after humble prayer recognized this call as God's voice through his Church, not as the voice of a particular party within the Church.

But what may the businessman ask? Certainly if a firm is offering the public a worthy service of some kind, he may ask for the success of his efforts, but he may not ask for the acceptance of his bid as against his rival's bid when both are offering an equally valuable service.

For what may a housewife ask? Chiefly for that patience which is the loving fruit of seeing one's immediate task in the perspective of a whole life's contribution. Bishop Donald B. Aldrich, in his delightful anthology of prayer entitled *The Golden Book of Prayer* includes a very homely poem, "Prayers for Grace in Little Things." A housewife could scarcely do better than absorb its teaching. It reads:

LORD of all pots and pans and things; since I've no time
    to be
A saint by doing lovely things or watching late with Thee,
Or dreaming in the dawnlight or storming heaven's gates,
Make me a saint by getting meals, and washing up the
    plates.

Altho I must have Martha's hands, I have a Mary mind;
And when I black the boots and shoes, Thy sandals, Lord,
    I find.
I think of how they trod the earth, what time I scrub the
    floor;
Accept this meditation, Lord, I haven't time for more.

Warm all the kitchen with Thy love, and light it with
    Thy peace;
Forgive me all my worrying, and make all grumbling
    cease.
Thou Who didst love to give men food, in room or by the
    sea,
Accept this service that I do—I do it unto Thee.

These are but examples, but the point should be clear.
Actually, as we grow older, our prayers of personal peti-
tion grow less and less. We tend, if we mature at all, to
have more and more concern for the common good, and
less and less worry about our own particular needs. The
prayer from William Bright's great collection, *For Guid-
ance,* says about all that the maturing Christian is willing
to ask for himself: "Grant us, in all our doubts and un-
certainties, the grace to ask what thou wouldest have us
to do, that the Spirit of Wisdom may save us from all
false choices, and that in thy light we may see aright and
in that straight path may not stumble." Possibly the best
criterion of prayer is just this: you may ask for anything
which with a good conscience you could ask of a father
who is equally fond of all the rest of his children.

The conclusion of this section is the most famous point
of the Sermon. It is the Golden Rule: *Therefore all things
whatsoever ye would that men should do to you, do ye
even so to them: for this is the law and the prophets.* The
words of the Catechism are a little simpler, but the point
is just the same: "Do to all men as I would they should
do unto me."

This is all so familiar that we can easily overlook what it really says. It means that I am to place myself in the position of others that they will be treated exactly as they wish to be treated; that is, the way I would like to be treated in their place. To use the time-honored Sunday School illustration, the Golden Rule does not mean that since I like pumpkin pie I am to force pumpkin pie on everybody else. It means, rather, that I am to take great pains to find out whether or not my friend likes pumpkin pie, and if he does not like it, then I must make sure that he is never put in the position of having to be polite about it. This extremely down-to-earth illustration has always touched American children where they live; but the point for adults is just the same, although not quite so easy.

Voltaire is a good example of how it does not work. This gentleman was the thinnest skinned man in Europe; at the same time, however, he reveled in having one of the bitterest tongues and most caustic pens. The result was to make this monumental genius into a semicomic or semi-tragic figure, depending on one's attitude about mankind. The least one can say is that he was not a happy man. For grown-up people the Golden Rule requires nothing less than the endless exercise of compassion. A broken and tragically unhappy man—broken through his own folly— comes to you as a friend. What are you going to say to him? What does the Golden Rule require? Obviously it does not require approval of his folly. Such an attitude is treating him as less than a person. He did not come to you as a friend to be lied to or to be treated with the condescension people reserve for those who no longer matter. The best test is: What would you yourself want to hear from a wise and trusted friend were you in his position.

The practice of the Golden Rule imposes an awesome restraint on the human tongue. One may, I suppose, be sarcastic about ideas, but even that may be dangerous if human beings have become identified with these ideas. But to be sarcastic, to gossip about another human being is an absolute violation of the Rule.

Criticism, under the Golden Rule, is something in which one engages with great diffidence. There is simply no use in saying that we are offering constructive criticism. This just makes nonsense out of criticism; all criticism is destructive, or it would not be criticism. The point is how to destroy something which from your point of view ought to be destroyed without hurting the person whose act or thought you are criticizing.

First you do not have the right to express any criticism whatever. If it be a public matter, and you are concerned as a citizen, then you have a right, indeed an obligation, to criticize something you think to be bad for the public good; but there is generally little to be said for doing this in such a way as to convey the notion that you disapprove of a man as much as you disapprove of his ideas. Politicians, too, are human beings, and most of them are deeply responsive to the approval or disapproval of their fellow citizens. They, too, like to be liked.

If it is an ecclesiastical matter—and this is in many ways more difficult—the first thing we must ascribe to people holding views opposed to ours is honesty and decent motives. As has been pointed out before, there is no church or religious body in the world which is primarily an aid to sin. The problem of the churches is always one of methodology. Some are authoritarian in method, some are democratic in method, and some attempt to maintain a fine balance between the two—but the Golden Rule absolutely forbids any one school of methodology to impugne the morals of the religion of another school of whose methodology it disapproves. I should point out that at top levels of religion this very rarely happens. It is only far down the line where trouble starts. A bad Roman Catholic disapproves of a bad Baptist, and both of them join in disapproving a bad Episcopalian. It is to be noted that when a decent pagan comes along and modestly admits that he is just as much a Christian as any of these three I have cited, he is telling the exact truth. Remember, the decent pagan does not remotely pretend that he is as decent a Christian as Albert Schweitzer. We can always take for granted that there is within all religious groups a quality of self-criticism which will never, ultimately, permit any one of them to adopt officially a position contrary to the welfare of God's people.

The exceptions to this are, frankly, most difficult to handle. The Golden Rule works; and it works in the most practical terms among ordinary people. But what of the people who do not respond to such treatment? I wish I knew the exact answer. The saintly bishop's treatment of Jean Valjean was justified by its effect on Jean. Jean stole the bishop's service plates, and the bishop refused to betray him to the police. One might argue that Jean Valjean was in some ways an outstanding man. One could also argue that the same bishop could just as easily have done the same thing a number of times with a number of other people, from which the only possible benefit, apart from that on the bishop's soul, would be the purchase of a new set of plates each time.

The clergy are often asked for help by seemingly dubious characters; frankly, most often the money so earnestly begged for a necessary journey to take a job, or to get one's tools out of the pawnshop, or to feed one's children, is promptly spent at a local barroom. This, whatever it may do for the local economy, does not seem to do much for religion.

But these same clergy will tell you of the odd occasion when the most unlikely man has done exactly what he said he would do. In one instance, such a man not only returned the money, but for years afterward until his death sent a small monthly donation to enable the clergyman to do just the same sort of thing for somebody else. I recognize the necessity of the role of the police in a fallen world, but I am haunted always by the fact that St. Francis of Assisi did more for a fallen world than all the police forces in history put together.

I am torn between the practical consideration of helping what Mr. Doolittle calls the "undeserving poor" and the religious consideration which dictates helping my brother in need. He was frank to say that he did not know the exact answer as to the handling of this problem, but I must be equally honest and say that I know the exact reason why I do not know the answer. The reason is that my compassion is not yet sufficiently developed to be like my Lord, who *needed not that any should testify of man; for he knew what was in man.*

Eighteen

Enter ye in at the strait gate: for wide is the gate, and broad is the way, that leadeth to destruction, and many there be which go in thereat:

Because strait is the gate, and narrow is the way, which leadeth unto life; and few there be that find it.

Beware of false prophets, which come to you in sheep's clothing, but inwardly they are ravening wolves.

Ye shall know them by their fruits. Do men gather grapes of thorns, or figs of thistles?

Even so every good tree bringeth forth good fruit; but a corrupt tree bringeth forth evil fruit.

A good tree cannot bring forth evil fruit, neither can a corrupt tree bring forth good fruit.

Every tree that bringeth not forth good fruit is hewn down, and cast into the fire.

Wherefore by their fruits ye shall know them.

There is probably no other place in the Gospels, with the possible exception of the story of Nicodemus, in which the distinction between life and existence is so sharply drawn. That most of the people on earth are just existing rather than living is the common assumption of the New Testament. But that this form of existence which so many share is nothing other than a common mass movement toward destruction is rarely stated as baldly as this.

One pictures masses of people moving along a great, broad avenue, neither knowing where they are going, nor caring particularly; just moving along because everyone else is. It is a picture which even the sternest of the prophets would recognize—an endless round of working in order to eat, in order to sleep, in order to work, in order to eat, in order to sleep, day after day, year after year. It is not for nothing that the Scripture constantly likens us to sheep. People who have sentimental ideas about the attractiveness of sheep are just people who have never known them. Sheep are unstable, easily frightened, moving as a mass without any seeming evidence of individual choice in a direction. When frightened, they always, by instinctive reaction, huddle together.

This is equally true of frightened people. The insecure minorities in our country do exactly the same thing. It is the herd reaction—one which makes them as easily misled as led. It has long been noted that the easiest place for any individual to hide is in the midst of a crowd: a fact which, combined with the easy generalizations to which most of us are prone, means that the easiest thing lost on this earth is the individual. The Occidental notion that all Japanese look alike is balanced by the Japanese notion that all Occidentals look alike. Either notion is ridiculous, but both are understandable pictures of human reaction.

The rest of the dread saying only completes the picture. The sheep can so easily be led by anything which looks like a sheep. Similarly the mass of people are always prey to the false prophets who disguise themselves as members of the company, but who are actually, inwardly, desirous of only one thing—using or abusing the simple, thoughtless, trusting multitude. They are to the great mass of people what ravening wolves are to a flock of sheep.

The way to life is not the broad, easy way of the herd; it is the narrow, difficult, tortuous path made up by an endless series of personal decisions. The way is narrow, and the gate is equally narrow. Dean Inge used to observe that it was quite wide enough because there was never at any time a great multitude trying to get in. This difficult path has never been generally popular; frankly there is nothing in the Scripture which intimates that it ever will be. Religion is, after all, hard work, and is twenty-four-hour-a-day work. Any attempt to make it seem otherwise is basically dishonest. I did not say that it was joyless work; it is not. It is the most rewarding and satisfying work there is, but it is still work.

Take the very precepts we have been considering together. If I am to avoid murder by avoiding being angry with my brother, there is an endless guard that has to be set both on my heart and on my mind to keep me from thinking the thoughts or saying the words which lead to anger. This is a constant discipline, and yet it is only one very small portion of the things which Jesus requires of me if I am to be complete. All the other precepts require attention too; whether I am at work or at play, there is always that self-conscious control which with God's help I must exercise day and night.

In common morality the herd mind will excuse all sorts of actions because they are customary or because everyone does them. I am told that it is a very difficult thing for an honest man to put in an honest expense account if he is traveling in the company of a number of other salesmen or representatives from his own office. The sheer pressure of belonging is so great that he does not want to let down his colleagues; yet if he puts in an absolutely honest account, the result is not going to be quite as one might expect. He is not really going to hurt his colleagues, because the company expects, and almost requires, that these accounts be padded.

No sensible man pretends that politicians have an easy time in life. More often than not they are confronted with choices which are incapable of a positive moral solution. In a particular city, for example, a very serious problem of adjustment exists for one portion of the population. The situation is so bad that it has become a national scandal, and everyone agrees that something ought to be done about it. Actually only one body is doing anything about it, and that happens to be one particular Christian denomination. The city fathers are as anxious as anyone else that something positive be done, but consider their position. If they support the one institution that is doing anything about it, they are immediately exposed to the charge of favoring one particular religious group—which in this country is political suicide.

If, on the other hand, they set up some broad and representative committee which, although it accomplishes nothing, at least does not put them in an untenable position, they will have at best avoided a possible problem, but actually will have succeeded in solving none. How can a man be honest in such a situation? The simple answer, I am afraid, is that he simply cannot be honest. He must get out of the situation before he can have any hope of doing what he thinks ought to be done, and by that time he may have lost the political power to act.

If I seem to be portraying a series of almost hopeless situations, it is only because they are the situations under which men have to work out their own "straight and narrow." A man may not have to live with the members of one firm forever nor with his fellow citizens of one community forever, but he is going to have to live with himself forever. The one transparent fact is that if one is going to have to live with oneself forever, then it is supremely important that one have a self worth living with: here lies the problem. Basically, although we approach God in the context of our life with our friends and our concern for them, our relationship with God is still an intimate and profoundly personal affair. Therefore we have to have a self sufficiently unified to be able to deal with a God who is, above all, One.

As I have intimated before, there is really no difficulty in having three or four selves. The problem lies in having one self. Probably in all Western history no man has equaled the Renaissance man in his ability to have three or four selves existing inside the same body. Take, for example, the Tudors. Any single Tudor was a combination of great intellectual power combined with profound theological interest; of sensualism combined with an almost fantastic taste in elegance of dress and surroundings; of profound faith in the destiny of one's people combined with a cynical evaluation of most of the individuals involved; of tremendous tenderness toward the simple and of arrogance bordering on cruelty toward the great and powerful.

The Tudors (particularly Henry VIII, Mary, and Elizabeth), in common with the Medicis (particularly Cosimo and Catherine), the Valois (particularly Francis I and Henry III), and the Hapsburgs (particularly Charles V and Philip II), were black and white people. The white was very white; and the black was very black. They were fascinating people and are thrilling to read about; but how difficult it would be to pick any one of them and say which one of his five or six totally different natures constituted the real person—the real self!

I do not think it is as easy as saying that they just had well-rounded personalities. I think it is rather that they had a number of personalities all inside one body; which personality was going to prevail at any one time would depend on the stimulus. All of them were, as might well be expected, totally unpredictable.

You and I are not Tudors. Many of us have neither their virtues nor their vices, neither their brains nor their blind spots; but in our own way, in our own context and setting, most of us have a rather alarming number of different selves all fighting with each other. We may be loving or

unloving with our friends, loving or unloving with our
families, loving or unloving with our enemies, broad-
minded and narrow-minded about those with whom we
differ, just or unjust depending on our power; but how
rarely are we consistent in our treatment of friends, family,
enemies, opponents, and dependents! All of us know the
tragicomic story of the New England funeral at which,
after great numbers of people had paid flowery tributes to
the virtues of the deceased, his widow asked her son to
look in the coffin and be sure it was his father they were
talking about! This, in its trivial way, is exactly what I
mean. So often with our families we are cold, unappreci-
ative, and so bored as to be uninteresting; whereas in public we may well glitter with all the humor, charm, and
refinement of polite society. The contrast is so great that
we only honestly describe ourselves as being different
people in the situations mentioned.

This is all common to the herd. After the herd animals
have brought forth their young and cared for them the
necessary amount of time, there seems to be no sign of
family affection whatever. None of the sheep will go
looking for a lost sheep. An animal that falls is left
behind, and there seems to be not the slightest care. Great
masses of people can exhibit this same quality. The identical crowd which is good-natured on the Fourth of July
may turn into a savage mob a few days later. Admiral
Dewey once said that triumphal arches ought always to
be built of bricks in order to give the populace something
to throw at the hero after he had gone through. It is not
as though the crowd at one time expressed the belief of

one of its members, and at another time the belief of another of its members; rather, it is that both members believe one thing at one time and another thing at another time. The crowd travels on the broad way, and it leads to destruction.

In a penetrating essay on medieval heresy, one learned historian has pointed out that the real damage done was not the torture and death of a few thousand people, but what the torturing and the death-dealing did to the people responsible. It takes no effort, no conscience, no choice to walk this road, but the longer one walks it, the harder it is going to be to change its pattern when one finally, here or hereafter, is forced to meet and to choose life.

But how may we know the straight and narrow? How may we recognize the people who will lead us to it? False prophets will in speech and in promises be as fully, if not more fully, gifted as true prophets. We have seen this often in the world of government. We have seen it even more often in the world of social economics, but we must not forget that Jesus is speaking of the world of religion, and that is where it hurts.

The day has passed when one has to defend fasting. Most Christians and all of the insurance companies consider fasting as quite acceptable. Admittedly this is not always for a religious reason, unless one considers religion in its very broadest aspects—that a disciplined body has a direct relationship with a disciplined soul. But what are we to think of the parson who urges a strict fast on his people, when we discover that his own form of fasting is merely the substitution of a rich fish diet for a rich meat diet? What are we to think when we discover that the man who has moved our hearts so deeply about missions really considers that his exhortation is all the contribution toward missions he himself is called upon to make? What shall we think of the man who deprecates gossip in a parish, and yet associates himself with the cruel allegations and imputations which party spirit in the Church can so often engender? How shall we assess the man who demands that the layman give up everything for Christ, and yet is himself most desperately protective about his day off and his privacy? What shall we say of the man who for popularity's sake offers men a religion less than the best he knows because the best he knows will not be popular? How shall we know who is telling the truth?

The cold common sense of Jesus provides an answer which has never been very popular. We know the leaders of men by their fruits. Rasputin had power, even great spiritual power, but judged by his friuts, what was he? Pelagius had power, a power which still affects the minds of men; but judged by his fruits, what was he? The clergy at the Salem witchcraft trials had power and popular support. What was the fruit? All of these men were, in their own way, false prophets—good for nothing; they were corrupt trees to be cut down and cast into the fire. A thorn bush does not produce grapes, and figs cannot be gathered from thistles. One knows a type of tree by the kind of fruit it produces. If you are going to be good, you are going to have to do good.

Even to use the phrase "do good" in our day is somewhat misleading. One of the worst things a man can be called nowadays is a "do-gooder." In common with most terms of opprobrium, it is now useful for disqualifying not only the unthinking sentimentality of thoughtless emotionalism, but also almost every constructive effort to solve the world's problems.

It can now be used comfortably to impugn the motives or morals of any positive force with whose methodology one disagrees. All this may be very useful, but it tends to confuse the real issue. The real issue is simply this: You cannot be a Christian without doing good. No phrase, no association of ideas, no political or social implications may be permitted to obscure this.

The Quakers came to this country with a deep concern, and they met the solid ill will of a number of their fellow countrymen. Their religion was held to be bogus and their actions ridiculous. Yet in season and out of season, in good times and bad, through wars in which they might not be participants and peace which these peaceful folk recognized as being nothing but armed truces, their quiet and unostentatious doing of the works of mercy have given them a secure position in the hearts of all men.

In the nineteenth century many people ridiculed the Salvation Army. Blasphemous and unfunny songs were made up about its members; the Salvationists were pelted with everything the human hand could reach—and the human hand can reach some very strange things. But the First World War ended all that. Their fruits made them known for the sort of people they really are.

I remember as a small boy coming home from school with a classmate, and as we passed a Roman Catholic church, to my fascinating amazement he told me of all the wicked and terrible things that went on inside the building, and that there was a secret store of weapons there so that when the right time came they could take over the whole country. I promptly went home and told my mother, who then and there for the only time in her life gave me what Cornelia Otis Skinner calls "the mother and father of a dressing-down." I do not think I ever saw her so coldly furious. The facts of life were explained to me in short order, and she promptly had one of her Roman Catholic friends take me to a Roman Catholic church to say my prayers. This ended this nonsense forever as far as I was concerned, but to my complete astonishment, forty-odd years later I still run across similar libels. Yet Father Damien, Cardinal Mercier, and Baron von Hügel are fruits of this tree.

And what about Jews themselves?—some of whom are lineal descendants of the very people who heard the original Sermon. When we think of Jews, do we think in terms of Nazi caricatures? Do we tell stories which are so funny when told by Jews themselves, and become so brutal when repeated by their enemies? Do we disguise our envy of their industriousness by objecting to their wealth and their power? Admittedly one may have a right to expect all Jews to be perfect just as one in theory has a right to expect all Christians to be; but this is hardly a realistic approach for either group. We will do much better to remember that two-thirds of all we know about God comes from the ancient Hebrews; that there is scarcely a learned Christian in the Western world who does not feel his soul enlarged by the piety and thinking of Martin Buber; and we will probably do best to remember that it was a Hebrew woman who gave birth to the Preacher on whose Sermon we are meditating.

In our complex world it is wiser to consider the best fruit the tree produces than to meditate endlessly on the worst. God, in history, takes care of the pruning. Possibly if we change the illustration slightly and think of each religious body as a separate stand of trees with some good and some bad in each, we will come nearer to the real point. We can, in that manner, avoid making the easy judgments common to the crowd. It is a wearisome process, but it is essential. One very good method is to keep a mental ledger. When someone of my own Church takes a public stand which can produce nothing but great embarrassment for the rest of us, I suspend all thinking on the matter until some member of another Communion takes an equally absurd stand. Over the years, this has helped to keep my thinking under control, but the real problem is not balancing out faults, it is balancing bad with good in the same institution.

For example, a great ecclesiastic in one Communion will issue a public statement so bigoted and anachronistic as to leave one astonished that he could hold so great a position. Taken as an isolated fact, the statement is so bad as to make one wonder if it could possibly be the official position of his Church. At such a time it is important to remember that just about six hundred miles to the north of that great ecclesiastic's city, another great ecclesiastic of the same Communion most generously provides one of his ancient churches for the exclusive use of a group whom the first prelate would regard as not just schismatic, but as out-and-out heretics.

This sort of knowledge will keep us from confusing the trees. If we can find this much variety within Christianity itself, it is really small wonder that the world at large moves so easily on the broad highway to destruction.

Nineteen

Again the voice of Jesus is lowered, and he speaks with a prophetic sorrow to his close friends:

Not every one that saith unto me, Lord, Lord, shall enter into the kingdom of heaven; but he that doeth the will of my Father which is in heaven.

Many will say to me in that day, Lord, Lord, have we not prophesied in thy name? and in thy name have cast out devils? and in thy name done many wonderful works?

And then will I profess unto them, I never knew you: depart from me, ye that work iniquity.

The easiest thing in the world is to recognize Jesus as Lord, and yet do nothing about it. The entire history of Christianity is shot through with examples. Jesus was scarcely dead on the Cross before some men were proclaiming that Jesus himself could not have had a real body, because something was said to be wrong about bodies. Bodies are the things which express sin; therefore, they reasoned, they must be the things which cause sin, so

obviously Jesus could not have had a real body. It is true
that they acknowledged him as Lord, but in their per-
verse thinking they had denied the very creative work of
God. It is not the Father's will that one should despise
his creation.

Men developed harshness and self-righteousness in
every form, and yet proclaimed the Lord of love as their
Lord, while denying his sovereignty by their every act.
Because of the tremendous political and social changes involved in the sixteenth- and seventeenth-century struggles,
we have come to think of the Reformation or the Counter
Reformation as being the only time in history when
conscientious men got busy tidying up the Church. This
is an understandable but inaccurate point of view. The
New Testament itself has the first account of such struggles, and the controversies in the Early Church are witness
to the constancy of the prophetic and reforming spirit.

We forget that Athanasius was not pleading the majority's case when he spoke out for an orthodoxy which would
assert the full reality of God's Incarnation. John Chrysostom was literally walked to death by brutal soldiers
because he insisted that orthodox rulers who called Jesus
"Lord" should, first of all, be decent people doing the
manifest will of the Father in Heaven. Bernard and Francis were reformers pleading for the exercise of holiness
and godly living among people who did not remotely deny
that Jesus was Lord. Wycliffe and Huss were no more
fiercely critical of the Church in their day than was Grosse-
teste. Erasmus and Colet were as brutally critical of
superstition as was Luther himself, and this comes down

to our own day with the prophets of our own time.

After the fourth century it was easier to call Jesus "Lord" than to deny it. Everybody did so; but the basic moral response which this statement should call forth was, time and again, sadly lacking. "Jesus" was in reality just a name substituted for "Osiris," "Apollo," "Thor," or "Woden." Over the protests of the friars, the same savage butcheries in religion's name which had so sullied the ancient civilizations of Mexico and Peru were continued under their conquerors, only this time done in the name of Jesus. Some of the saintliest men in the world were involved in the proceedings of the Star Chamber, and yet apparently saw little wrong with it. The suppression of the Old Believers in Russia was accomplished with a relentless savagery which has rested uneasily on the conscience of the Russian Church ever since. The Old Believers were, from my point of view, entirely wrong, but the method used in suppressing them was so wrong as to make the original wrong seem right. The New England conscience felt no twinges about flogging Quakers or hanging witches; yet it would have insisted that both were done because Jesus was Lord. The treatment of the Mormons in the nineteenth century was brutal beyond belief. And what of the pogroms which have gone on for centuries—the wholesale persecution of Jews by people who acknowledged Jesus as "Lord"?

A righteous man does righteously. A man who acknowledges Jesus is supposed to behave like Jesus. The thought of Jesus being involved in the instances I have cited is so revolting to the human mind that there have often been decent people who were willing to behave like Jesus insofar as they could, but who would not acknowledge him as Lord if this meant that they would have to behave like the Christians they saw around them. The phrase which was so moving in the days of the martyrs—"See how these Christians love one another"—was ultimately turned into the coldest irony when it came from the mouths of Turkish soldiers watching competing Christian Communions riot around the Church of the Holy Sepulcher.

The tragedy is that many of these people were sincere people. They honestly believed that they had prophesied in Jesus' name, and in his name had cast out devils and done great works. But the judgment is inexorable, "I never knew you. Go away. Your works are evil."

Human logic is never an adequate substitute for the human heart. One can, in terms of strict logic, justify almost any type of persecution, and this logic may not have one single "logical" flaw in it. The only trouble is that it is not true. A child could pick the basic flaw. The flaw lies in the premise. As one greathearted Christian wrote to Calvin: "To burn a man is not to prove a doctrine; it is to burn a man." No logic, no expediency, no urgency, no fear in the world can justify the killing spirit of the Destroyer.

One remembers Jesus' anger when James and John wanted to call down a fire from heaven to consume the Samaritans. Jesus turned and rebuked them with the stern reminder: *Ye know not what manner of spirit ye are of. For the Son of Man is not come to destroy men's lives, but to save them.* This passage must always cause great heart-searching for the clergy. Too many of us remember the terrifying legend of the Grand Inquisitor in Dostoevski's *The Brothers Karamazov.* Were one able to dismiss the legend as just an attack on fifteenth-century Spanish religion, it might be one thing; but it is not that easy. It is an attack on the constant tendency of all portions of the Christian Church to require of men things which Jesus did not require, and to use methods which Jesus, after careful thought, had forgone: it is to treat Jesus as an abstract idea instead of a person.

This problem, however, is not one confined exclusively to the clergy. Most people in your own community judge your own church not by its prayer book or lack of it, not by its official statements or lack of them, not by your church's power or wealth or lack of them, but by what you are like as an individual human being representing your brand of Christianity. "Lord, Lord" is just not good enough.

Twenty

Therefore whosoever heareth these sayings of mine, and doeth them, I will liken him unto a wise man, which built his house upon a rock:

And the rain descended, and the floods came, and the winds blew, and beat upon that house; and it fell not: for it was founded upon a rock.

And every one that heareth these sayings of mine, and doeth them not, shall be likened unto a foolish man, which built his house upon the sand:

And the rain descended, and the floods came, and the winds blew, and beat upon that house; and it fell: and great was the fall of it.

It seems transparently clear that there is a profound distinction between hearing and doing on one hand, and hearing and not doing on the other. Yet, most of us have a basic tendency to ask for good advice, get it, and then not to follow it. Were we to examine carefully what we are actually doing, we would discover that most of the time we are not really asking for advice at all; we are just seeking support for something which is already completely decided in our own minds.

My physician friends tell me that one of the endless problems in helping people to reduce their weight is that of persuading them that the chief way to reduce weight is simply to eat less. Fad after fad have been introduced in the whole matter of dieting, but when reduced to their basic essentials, all they really tend to do is to permit people to eat as much as they want of food they do not want, and thus accomplish the desired end by self-deception. Recognizing all the associated problems and the possible necessity of medication, the way to stop drinking is to stop. The way to stop smoking is to stop. Whether individuals really desire to do either of these things may be a totally different matter.

Bishop Manning used to assert that the rarest thing in life was for anyone to agree with somebody else's opinion. All the average man does is agree when somebody else states the opinion he already holds.

For a third of my life I have listened to bursts of applause in the middle of speeches at various functions; such applause is audible evidence of the correctness of the Bishop's statement. A magnificent speech is not a speech which raises questions or provokes thought, it is a speech which says in brilliant or amusing terms all the things which the audience already believes to be true, which is brutally or amusingly rude to all the enemies common to the audience, and which concludes with some splendid cliché upholding the eternal rightness and value

of the audience's continuing to be exactly the way it is
at the moment.

This is as true of Church congress addresses as it is of
political speeches or after-dinner harangues. Yet all of
this has only to do with advice. What of something which
is not offered as advice at all? Take the very word of truth
itself. Too often we have forgotten this concluding portion
of the Sermon on the Mount, and have gone our kindly,
sentimental way, assuming that Jesus was just being
sweet and helpful and offering good advice. But he is not
offering advice at all. He is explaining the facts of life,
and we either do it and live, or do not do it and continue
in our deadliness.

With life we cannot either take it or leave it; we take
it or it leaves us. The Sermon on the Mount is the blueprint of completeness. There are certain things in this
world which just have to be treated as settled and no
longer open to opinion: for example, the function of a
candlestick is to hold a candle. The stick may take any
shape imaginable, but it must have a socket or a spike
which will hold a candle upright: this is not even open
to debate. A bowl still has to have sufficient breadth and
depth to hold something. It may be large or small, regular
or irregular in shape, but the basic definition still stands.

Jesus was not engaged in philosophic musing, nor even
in pious meditation; he was speaking with urgency the
words of life. To hear his words and to do them is to
build securely; to hear the words and not to do them
is finally to destroy whatever building has previously gone
on. Solid building has, in our day, become a matter of

great concern. We speak of "building in depth" when we mean to imply the necessity of having a secure foundation, rather than peripheral support. We are concerned that our children are growing up in an undisciplined world, that we have not provided them with the inner resources to get them through the difficult moments in life. Our magazines are filled with articles expressing grave concern over the lack of internal security manifested by some of our men when they were prisoners of war.

First, I think we should always admit in honesty that it is considerably easier to write an article about the insecurity of a prisoner of war than it is to be one and remain secure. But quite apart from that, the real difficulty is that though some held out nobly, others seemed scarcely to struggle before giving in. When I was a young man I was aware of the astonishing weaknesses shown up in our system at the time of the 1929 stock-market crash. It was clear that some of our fellow citizens had invested so completely in this world and its values that when this world collapsed, an individual's values had to collapse with it.

More recently we have been troubled by the intellectual plottings of two men who have made us profoundly aware of the increasing dangers of "conformity" and "give-up-itis." We are now being warned that individual initiative and individual responsibility are fast disappearing, chiefly from the sheer pressure of "belonging." All the junior executives in one industry will be required to wear the same type of clothing, live in the same type of house, own the same type of car, and what is more serious, think the same type of thought and go to the same type of church.

Whereas individualism used to be rugged, now the only individualism there is seems to be ragged, and I am not sure this is a total improvement. To pursue Jesus' illustration, just what is going to happen when trouble comes to Mortgage Hill? First of course the houses are going to go, then the furniture, then the automobile, then the TV set, and lastly the refrigerator. The mere fact that two-thirds of the world manages to do without most of these things is not going to be of much comfort, because we are not giving our own people the resources to get them over the rough places. The fall of the house built on sand is always tragically devastating.

The crash is one that is far from local in its effect. It is so far from being localized that our entire nation and people suffer. It is not very helpful to make moralistic observations at the expense of people caught in an almost unbreakable pattern, but as a Christian and a clergyman I must hope that the words of Jesus can still get through to the point that people chained to the outward forms of their manner of living may yet hear him, and in the secret places of the heart make a space where they can live as free men.

Our popular conformism certainly has its humorous side —a side which both our friends and enemies abroad are always pleased to point out. The earnest American tourist, complete with sunglasses, shorts, camera, and light meter, has become a regrettable comic figure the world over. Our humorous pursuit of "culture," at which Mark Twain poked gentle fun, has now become a hallmark as easily identifiable in Kyoto as in Paris.

The late Helen Hokinson portrayed another standard brand of American—the aging and really quite likable perennial college graduate of one of the country's better women's colleges. One of my dear old friends used to be immensely flattered by being shown again and again in Miss Hokinson's cartoons. The endearing thing was that she regarded all these cartoons as sketches of important calendar events, rather than essays in humor. But these gentle and often most lovable characteristics do not portray the qualities which provoke the sardonic and often deadly humor of our enemies. Sardonic humor delights in pointing out that whereas our history is the account of a nation grown great by open debate, town meeting, and individual initiative, the honest picture of our people today is of a great nation convincing itself that security is the only thing which matters, and then proceeding to define security as protective care from the cradle to the grave.

It is not by accident that Jesus uses an illustration applicable to an individual man. It is as individual men and women that we survive or fall. Security, from Jesus' point of view, is the inevitable fruit of a right relationship with God and man. The good life can never be sought for its own sake; it is the by-product of righteousness. By this I mean that if one takes on righteousness solely for the purpose of being secure, one is going to become both unrighteous and insecure. Security is a gift of God and in the long run has absolutely no meaning until the day when we are faced with what the world regards as insecurity: death.

Then it is that real strength shows. At this point it would be well to hear the words of one who had good reason to know the difference between worldly and otherworldly security. His words have to be taken seriously because they are a preview of the remainder of his life. St. John Chrysostom died because of his opposition to the imperial family. The touching account of his patience under his sufferings, his gentleness to the brutal soldiers, and his joyful laying down of his tired body gave credence to his exposition of this phrase.

" 'For the rain descended,' saith he, 'the floods came, the winds blew, and beat upon that house; and it fell not: for it was founded upon the rock.'

"By 'rain' here, and 'floods,' and 'winds,' he is expressing metaphorically the calamities and afflictions that befall men; such as false accusations, plots, bereavements, deaths, loss of friends, vexations from strangers, all the ills in our life that any one could mention. 'But to none of these,' saith he, 'doth such a soul give way; and the cause is, it is founded on the rock.' He calls the steadfastness of his doctrine a rock; because in truth his commands are stronger than any rock, setting one above all the waves of human affairs. For he who keeps these things strictly, will not have the advantage of men only when they are vexing him, but even of the very devils plotting against him. And that it is not vain boasting so to speak. Job is our witness, who received all the assaults of the devil, and stood unmoveable; and the apostles too are our witnesses, for that when the waves of the whole world were beating against them, when both nations and princes, both their own people and strangers, both the evil spirits, and the devil, and every engine was set in motion, they stood firmer than a rock, and dispersed it all.

"And now, what can be happier than this kind of life? For this, not wealth, not strength of body, not glory, not power, nor ought else will be able to secure, but only the possession of virtue. For there is not, nay there is not another life we may find free from all evils, but this alone. And ye are witnesses, who know the plots in king's courts, the turmoils and the troubles in the houses of the rich. But there was not among the apostles any such thing.

"What then? Did no such thing befall them? Did they suffer no evil at any man's hand? Nay, the marvel is this above all things, that they were indeed the object of many plots, and many storms burst upon them, but their soul was not overset by them, nor thrown into despair, but with naked bodies they wrestled, prevailed, and triumphed.

"Thou then likewise, if thou be willing to perform these things exactly, shalt laugh all ills to scorn. Yea, for if thou be but strengthened with such philosophy as is in these admonitions, nothing shall be able to hurt thee. Since in what is he to harm thee, who is minded to lay plots? Will he take away thy money? Well, but before their threatening thou wast commanded to despise it, and to abstain from it so exceedingly, as not so much as even to ask any such thing of thy Lord. But doth he cast thee into prison? Why, before thy prison, thou wast enjoined so to live, as to be crucified even to all the world. But doth he speak evil? Nay, from this pain also Christ hath delivered thee, by promising thee without toil a great reward for the endurance of evil, and making thee so clear from the anger and vexation hence arising, as even to command thee to pray for them. But doth he banish thee and involve thee in innumerable ills? Well, he is making the crown more glorious for thee. But doth he destroy and murder thee? Even hereby he profits thee very greatly, procuring for thee the rewards of the martyrs, and conducting thee more quickly into the untroubled haven, and affording thee matter for a more abundant recompence, and contriving for thee to make a gain of the universal penalty. Which thing indeed is most marvellous of all, that the plotters, so far from injuring at all, do rather make the objects of their despite more approved. To this what can be comparable? I mean, to the choice of such a mode of life as this, and no other, is."

St. John's exegesis has the authentic ring which comes from a man who really knows what he is talking about. For him, as for Christians everywhere, Jesus is not only master builder, but he is the rock on which the building stands. St. Paul was to note this: with reference to building, he said that no man can lay any of the foundation, for the foundation is already laid—Jesus Christ. In another place St. Paul calls Jesus "the chief corner stone." When he does so, he is fully conscious of the phrase in the Psalms: *The stone which the builders refused is become the head stone of the corner.*

Thus, from the Christian point of view, Jesus himself is Man's criterion of security. His very name means, "God saves." But the title is so beautiful that we are apt to forget that the next question is the quite reasonable one: "God saves us from what?" To be fair to the Hebrew mind, one would probably have to say first that God saves *to* himself. For the practical-minded Hebrew it was clear enough that man was not designed to be subject to the world, the flesh, and the devil, but rather subject only to God. From Jesus' point of view, the world, the flesh, and the devil were of the domain of existence, but not of life.

It is against this background that we must read that thoughtful answer which Jesus sent back to John Baptist when the latter asked from prison to find out who Jesus really was. It was a public question asked publicly, and one which had to be answered publicly. Therefore Jesus formulated an answer which would convey the true facts to John. John was to weigh seriously every word he said: "Go and show John the things you hear and see: the blind are receiving their sight; the lame are walking; and the lepers are being cleansed; the deaf are hearing, the dead are becoming alive; and the poor are having the Gospel preached to them."

In this list Jesus was not furnishing John with a list of miracles. John was a great prophet who was fully aware of the fact that miracles were common to all prophets and to many other sons of Israel. Such a list would not necessarily impress John Baptist in the slightest unless he was aware, as was Jesus, that the ultimate problem of religion is not the physically blind, or the physically old, or the physically unclean, or the physically deaf, or the physically dead, or the poverty-stricken, but that the ultimate problem of religion is the great mass of people who suffer from all of these complaints in a spiritual sense.

It was to all of these people that Jesus preached, and it was from these, who were honest enough to know their situation, that he received his warmest support. The Pharisees of any age are not so often wicked men as they are determinedly blind and deaf men. They will not see; they will not hear. The vast congregation of humanity has not changed much.

Francis of Assisi was regarded as a saint by the humble and confused and unloved people of his day, but his order was viewed with profound suspicion by diocesan authorities. The Welsh miners heard John Wesley; most of his brother clergy did not. The American Indians understood the Quakers; but the Puritans did not and would not.

It is certainly not our business to assess and evaluate facts which have not yet passed into that judgmental and selective catalogue of events we call history; but many people in all Communions have watched with sympathy the struggle of the French Worker Priests to minister to a religiously almost forgotten segment of the French populace.

Jonathan Swift's acidulous comment is, it seems to me, in order: "There's none so blind as those who will not see."

Twenty one

*And it came to pass, when Jesus had enaed these sayings,
the people were astonished at his doctrine:*

*For he taught them as one having authority, and not
as the scribes.*

I have presumed at the beginning of this book to make
a new translation of a portion of this text. It is not an
elegant translation, but it at least has the virtue of conveying to modern readers some of the forthright quality of
the "Good News" as men of the first century heard and
read it.

"The crowd were greatly struck by his teaching for he
taught them as one having the right to." The authentic
quality of Jesus' personality comes through in this passage. It illustrates the timeless difference between the
Prophet and the Scribe. The Scribes of all churches in all
ages have had to lean on someone else's personal knowledge to give credence to their conclusions.

Scribes are really quite necessary people, for it is due

to their faithful transmission of what they receive that succeeding generations are enabled to learn from the past. The danger, of course, is that the Scribe, out of this very faithfulness, can make a tomb out of something which is intended to be a springboard. The very Bible itself is Good News about a Person and how that Person works. It is not, nor was it intended to be, a textbook in physics or astronomy. The Bible uses its own language, and its own thought forms to convey its own ideas, but these are ideas to be observed from within and not from without. To try to read the Bible and disregard the community which tested it by living is to expect animation in a vacuum.

The Bible only makes its real impact on people who already know it is true before they start reading. If I have not already come to discern the hand of a living Lord both in my life and in the lives of those around me, then reading the Bible is not really going to have any more effect on me than the reading of any other charming and occasionally quaint history of men's reactions.

In all fairness, the Scribe preserved the words, which is no small thing; but he has often obscured the Word by his finespun reasoning. The popular fiction that medieval scholasticism degenerated into speculation as to how many angels could dance on the point of a needle pales before the record of some of the exponents of nineteenth-century Biblicism. At no point does this become worse than in the time-honored urge to treat an illustration as though it were a definitive thesis replete with hidden symbolism.

The two best-known parables in the New Testament have suffered the most by this treatment. The Parable

of the Good Samaritan, which was propounded for the
sole purpose of pulling out of the listener an adequate
definition of neighborliness, has for centuries been man-
handled into a mystical account of man's passage through
life, including penance, absolution, and the Second Advent.
The Parable of the Prodigal Son, which was told to press
the point that even a very earthly human father's forgiveness was so great that we could therefore expect much
more from the Father in Heaven, has been treated as an
attempted description of God, which it most certainly is
not. My own Communion prescribes as one of the Lenten
"Opening Sentences" this quotation from the Parable: "I
will arise and go to my father, and will say unto him,
Father, I have sinned against heaven, and before thee, and
am no more worthy to be called thy son." This is all very
well and deeply moving, until one remembers the context
and recalls that the Prodigal Son was not sorry, he was just
hungry. The speech itself has a calculated quality which
does nothing to make the Prodigal more attractive.

It is the Scribal mind at its worst which has produced
that popular distinction between "the spirit and the letter
of the law." This is, of course, exactly what St. Paul did
not mean. There is no such thing as the spirit of the law.
The choice was either the "spirit" or the "law." "Letter"
means "law," and from St. Paul's point of view, this was
the "ministry of death."

It is the Scribal mind which has the passion for re-
solving paradoxes; yet all religions in general and the
Christian religion in particular simply bristle with paradoxes which are resolved only in personal and never in

academic terms. There are no paradoxes in the mind of
God, but the integrity of that mind produces paradoxes
in our differing reactions to its insistent drive.

In our personal lives we have to face the paradox of love
and judgment. There are things so wicked that the dread
holiness of God will not tolerate doing; yet, at the same
time, God loves the wicked as much as he loves the righteous. These are the facts of life we have to live. In the
ultimate sense, love and judgment are one and the same
thing; but in the immediate sense one hurts and one heals.
It is this quality which gives the never-ending fascination
to that mystery of Jesus' suffering which we call the Passion, in which the tension between love and judgment is
met and resolved. To attempt to resolve this tension without recourse to the Way of the Cross is to be trivial with
both God and man.

The Prophet speaks the words of God directly. There is
always a complete lack of self-consciousness; in his statements he never attempts to justify God's point of view, nor
does he seem to have the slightest interest in making the
words conform with all the words uttered by all other
Prophets before him. He speaks as one having the right
to speak.

Dr. Frederick Grant has pointed out that we are hearing
the authentic tone of Jesus' voice in this Sermon if we
change the emphasis in the recurring phrase, *I say unto
you*. Centuries of piety have made us read it, "*I* say unto
you"; whereas what the crowd heard was "I *say* unto you."
We must not miss the point. The crowd heard him as a

Prophet, and up to the last minute of his trial, it was as a Prophet that Jesus was persecuted.

Prophets are always hard-hitting, but the persons hit hardest are not the simple, uninstructed, and often very confused mass of people, but the entrenched ecclesiastical and civil authorities, and the tragic group who have moved over from the proclamation of God's righteousness to the position of self-righteousness.

The common people heard Jesus gladly. They always do when they have any chance to hear him. As a professional Christian I recognize only too well in myself all the qualities of Scribal religion. Men ask me for bread and I always give it to them; but unless I am very careful, it is bread so dehydrated for preservation as to seem to them exactly like a stone.

When men ask to see Jesus I must do a lot more than hand them a book. I have to show them a person. My usefulness is somewhat limited if I have never met him. To be a guardian of culture and chaplain to the status quo will accomplish little save the preservation of the world's antiquarian interests and the imparting to ordinary men and women of a fixed conviction that religion has every gift in the world save relevance.

Epilogue

This Sermon on the Mount is part of the initial thrust which resulted in completely changing the minds of men. Scribal religion of every age and of every faith is a religion of rules; therefore the moral man to the Scribe is the man who breaks no rules. Thus moral reformation in the Old Testament means a "new look." The Sermon on the Mount is not the requirement of a new look, but of a new creature. It is to be noted that not even the Holy Apostles themselves were able to follow the precepts of the Sermon on the Mount until something else had happened. They had to be born again—born of the Spirit—and for the renewing of that Spirit within them a terrible price had to be paid and this world's ultimate tension resolved.

The Sermon does not stand apart from its Preacher. We only know of the Sermon because of its Preacher. The Preacher had to live out that Sermon, had to suffer and die and live again in order for it to make its full sense.

Christians have found him to be God's original blueprint for man: what God had in mind when man was created. It was from the contemporary realization that he was the express image of the Immortal Father's face that men came to see the fullness of that At-one-ment which turned out to be their redemption.

There are many theories of the Atonement, and none is without its own important insight, but for people not specially trained in theology many of them may seem mutually contradictory and needlessly confusing. One thing, however, must be recognized immediately, or there really cannot be any such thing as a Christian understanding of the Atonement. Jesus did not come to save us from God the Father; God, in the fullness of time, sent forth his Son, and in Jesus, man, by his own free loving acceptance of the Father's will, is recalled to his original pattern and vocation. Jesus is the Redeemer in that he recovers from captivity the lost and the alienated. It is the manumission of a slave race.

The love of God so shows itself in Jesus on the Cross that all of us can discern, however weakly, the saving mercy of our God. To take on Jesus is to be reconciled with God and man. As St. Paul explains, "He is our peace." Belonging to him means being in him, and the whole power of St. Paul's writing lies in his profound understanding of the new man in Christ. Things between God, as he is, and me, as I am, have been put right by Jesus. Peacemaking is the most difficult and costly exploit of the human soul. It cost the love of God—nothing less than the Crucifixion of Jesus. It is so easy to get over into theory at this point that one must recall the fact that this is not theory about good and evil, but the personal relationships between God and man. William Porcher Du-Bose's paean, in his standard classic "The Soteriology of the New Testament," conveys more than all my descriptions and analyses could ever hope to:

"Present Peace, the feeling that there is now nothing between us and God; the possession already of a finished Salvation; the privilege and power of divesting our consciousness of every thought or feeling, but that 'my God, thou art good; my soul thou art happy'; the immediateness and absoluteness or unqualifiedness of the new relation of oneness established between us and God, by the sole act of Jesus Christ and independent of anything in us, save only our faith or personal acceptance and appropriation of it—how essential a spiritual attitude is this in the Christian life! To disturb it by exacting any condition whatsoever of ourselves, what is it but just so much to limit the freeness and fullness of the divine grace! No; I am disturbed by no sense of guilt for the past, by no 'consciousness-of-sin' in the present, by no fear of unfaithfulness or failure in the future.

"Any doubt or apprehension upon any one of these scores is to limit my Salvation and dishonour my Saviour. Since nothing but the limitation of our faith can limit God's grace, it is impossible to believe too much."

The Preacher of the Sermon is for me the Word of God incarnate. He is not a prophet; he is the One toward whose coming the prophets looked. His words, therefore, are not just the meditations of a religious genius, however useful;

they are the words of life itself spoken by him who is the Life. His words shed light because he himself is the Light; they point the way because he is the Way.

To be alive, to be able to see, and to know where we are going—is there anything else which matters? Not if the words are properly defined! To know the only true God, and Jesus Christ whom he has sent, is to have life eternal starting right here and now. To know ourselves and each other as bearers of the image of God is to see what Jesus really means to the life of men—to know him as God's word to us about ourselves. To know that we shall always be with the Lord is to know everything we need to know regarding our purpose for living. But we know even more than that: we know that God is not only beside us in the valley of the shadow—he is in us as we move through the valley. In St. Paul's glorious words, "to me to live is Christ"—and again, "I live; yet not I, but Christ liveth in me; and the life which I now live in the flesh I live by the faith of the Son of God, who loved me, and gave himself for me."

Christ speaks to us as one having the right to. In an age so tragically uncertain, he calls us to become what we really are—living, though latent, images of our God.

He serves man best
Who will not let him go 'til,
Beneath the earthy mask, he has
Discerned the living image of his God.

ABOUT THE AUTHOR

Edward N. West is Canon Sacrist of the Cathedral of St. John the Divine, New York City. A contributor to the *Encyclopedia Americana* and the author of numerous articles on ecclesiastical music and architecture, he has also written two books: *Meditations on the Gospel of St. John,* which was The Harper Book For Lent, 1955, and *The History of The Cross,* which was richly illustrated by the paintings of the well-known artist Norman Laliberte.

Born in Boston, Canon West studied at Boston University, General Theological Seminary, and Trinity College. Honorary degrees have been granted to him by Ripon College, Boston University, and the Russian Theological Institute in Paris.

For seven years Canon West was curate and rector of Trinity Church, Ossining, New York. During the same period, he was special preacher at Canterbury Cathedral in London at three different times, select preacher at the University of Dublin, honorary chaplain to the Archbishop of Canterbury at the Lambeth Conference in 1948, and Master of Ceremonies at the Anglican Conference in 1954.

Canon West's special interest in Biblical studies and his many years of devoted work in the pastoral ministry have given him unusual insight into the subject matter of this volume: the best-remembered and best-loved teachings of Christ, as contained in the Sermon on the Mount.

This book was set in Garamond

and Cloister Black types, printed,

and bound by The Haddon Craftsmen.

The Reverend Dr. Edward N. West is Canon Sacrist of the Cathedral of St. John the Divine in New York City. A leading liturgical and Biblical scholar, he has written two previous books, *Meditation on the Gospel of St. John* and *The History of the Cross,* and has contributed numerous articles to the *Encyclopedia Americana* and to national magazines.

(continued on back flap)